*Travels in the*
*Colonies in 1773-1775*

DESCRIBED IN THE LETTERS

OF WILLIAM MYLNE

# Travels in the Colonies in 1773-1775

DESCRIBED IN THE LETTERS

OF WILLIAM MYLNE

EDITED BY

Ted Ruddock

The University of Georgia Press   Athens and London

© 1993 by the University of Georgia Press
Athens, Georgia 30602
All rights reserved
Designed by Betty Palmer McDaniel
Set in 11 on 12½ Garamond #3
by Tseng Information Systems, Inc.

Library of Congress Cataloging in Publication Data

Mylne, William.
Travels in the colonies in 1773–1775: described in
the letters of William Mylne / edited by Ted Ruddock.
p. cm.
Includes bibliographical references (p.   ) and index.
ISBN 0-8203-1426-9 (alk. paper)
1. United States—Description and travel—To 1783.
2. Mylne, William—Correspondence.
I. Ruddock, Ted, 1930–    II. Title.
E163.M95   1993
917.304′27—dc20          91-37478
                          CIP

British Library Cataloging in Publication Data available

Documents in the Public Record Office, London,
are Crown Copyright and quoted by permission
of the Comptroller of HM Stationery Office.

Reissue published in 2021

Most University Press titles are available
from popular e-book vendors.

Printed digitally

ISBN 9780820359878 (Hardcover)
ISBN 9780820359885 (Paperback)
ISBN 9780820359861 (Ebook)

# Contents

Foreword to the Reissue
vii

Preface
xiii

CHAPTER 1
Introduction: Background to the Journeys
1

CHAPTER 2
Before Departure
10

CHAPTER 3
South Carolina and Georgia
19

CHAPTER 4
Charlestown to New York
61

CHAPTER 5
Return to Britain and End of Story
78

APPENDIX 1
William Mylne's Power of Attorney
89

APPENDIX 2
Calendar of Letters, 1773–1775
91

Main Sources
93

Annotated Index
97

## *Foreword to the Reissue*

When in December 1773 William Mylne, Scottish architect, builder, and master mason, arrived in Charleston in the colony of South Carolina, he was embarking on a challenging and unanticipated experience. Scots had been arriving in the colonies in significant numbers for more than half a century before Mylne set foot in Charleston. They had been encouraged to leave their homeland as part of the effort to secure colonial settlement, against the French and the Spanish and, of course, the Native population. Scottish Highland troops had been recruited in the 1730s to hold the southern frontier against the Spanish, and an exodus of Highland Scots at around the same time had established a flourishing settlement in the Cape Fear region of North Carolina.

Many Scots had done well in the colonies, particularly in the tobacco trade. By the end of the seventeenth century Scots were prominent as planters, factors, and traders. Indeed, by the time Mylne arrived in Carolina, Scots dominated the tobacco trade, and the exponential rise of the city of Glasgow was partly due to its success. Ironically, Mylne regretted a lack of Scottish-produced snuff in Carolina (Edinburgh, his home city, had many snuff mills) as he attempted to produce his own from local tobacco.

Mylne's career as an architect and builder was under way at a promising time for Edinburgh. Its medieval center was notoriously cramped, overcrowded, and insalubrious on its rocky spine—there was an urgent need for expansion. A New Town had been planned with a consequent demand for ambitious building work. Although, as documented by frequent newspaper reports, events and developments on the other side of the Atlantic held much interest in Scotland, it is unlikely that Mylne would have contemplated making his future in the colonies if he had not been forced by circumstance. We do not know how much he himself knew of those colonies and how Scots had fared, but it is clear that, bankrupt by disaster in his home city, he hoped that crossing the Atlantic would offer a means of restoring his fortunes. What is intriguing is that he did not think of using his skills and experience to contribute to the rapid expansion of American cities. He wanted to try his hand as a planter, and he wanted a period of solitude. It is not clear if he was aware that James Oglethorpe, first governor of the colony of Georgia, originally envisaged the colony as a place of refuge for debtors, although that intention did not materialize.

Mylne's planting aspirations eventually took him west to Augusta and on to Stephen's Creek, close to the Savannah River. He was helped along the way by fellow Scots. At times others resented what they felt to be Scottish "clannishness," which they saw as giving Scots an unfair advantage. Mylne's long-term aim was to acquire sufficient land to grow cash crops—corn, tobacco, indigo—with a workforce of three enslaved people and a servant girl brought from home. He had no reservations about either slavery or indentured labor and assumed that managing a plantation required both. The short-term reality was rather different from these aspirations. He occupied a rough cabin and struggled to supply himself with basic needs. Early frost destroyed his crops. For long periods his only company was his dog and his horse. His letters are contradictory, at the same time professing contentment with his basic, solitary existence and requesting from his sister in Scotland items that would make life more comfortable—tools, "half a dozen of good shirts" (41), sheets, and towels. He complains of inflated American prices, but he also prides himself on his ability to adjust. Like so many settlers, he had to learn basic survival skills and to hunt and forage to keep himself alive.

Mylne's letters describe his life in some detail and provide a valuable insight into the experience of a man whose early expectations were very different from the realities of pioneering in the colonies. He was a man escaping from and, to an extent, atoning for financial ruin, for which he accepts a degree of blame. A suggestion lurks in the tone of his letters that he sees hard work and solitude as a kind of self-correction. He was hoping for a new life in a new environment, but he did not have the means or the opportunities of those of his countrymen who were in a position to make fortunes. But neither was he one of the thousands who left Scotland with almost nothing, from economic necessity, or because they were forced from their homes. The colonies, and later the new republic of the United States of America, offered the potential to remake lives, and for Mylne that was the attraction, underpinned by a desire to seek anonymity. He did not want to be identified as the man responsible for a calamitous building project. He wanted to escape the small world of professional Edinburgh and disappear into American wilderness, although Scottish connectivity in Georgia remained important to him.

Mylne's arrival in South Carolina and Georgia coincided with growing tension in the colonies as resentment against British tax impositions grew. At the same time Indigenous nations resisted the colonists' attempts to expand westward as earlier agreements and borders were ignored. Once the frontier was secured against rival Europeans, it was the Indigenous peoples, in Georgia predominantly Cherokees and Creeks, who were seen as barriers to further settlement. By the 1770s there was a history of brutal attacks, authorized and otherwise, on the Native townships and reciprocal attacks on white settlements.

Mylne does not dwell on these troubles, though in a letter of September 1774 he writes, "We are to have peace here. A number of Indians have gone to settle matters with the Governor at Savannah" (53). He goes on to say that as there are no troops in the area, the Indians could easily have driven out the white population. By this time Mylne is realizing that his experiment has failed. At the end of that year he leaves Stephen's Creek.

As he makes his way on horseback north and east, to Wilmington, North Carolina (an area where many Scots settled), through Virginia and Maryland to Philadelphia and on to New Jersey, he sees everywhere preparations for war. In a letter to his sister of January 1775 he writes, "All the Americans seem obstinate not to make any concessions to England, in every place where I have been they talk of fighting to the last man for their liberties and properties"

(56). He worries at the possibility of "a general Indian war & a civil one" (56) erupting simultaneously but at the same time believes that British government troops would easily deal with any insurrection. He gives us a glimpse of the febrile atmosphere in the months leading to the Declaration of Independence. Scots would fight on both sides when war came.

William Mylne's American experience was not a success, but it perhaps better enabled him to return to Britain with the will to reestablish his career as a builder. Significantly, this did not happen in Scotland but in Ireland. He spent the rest of his life in Dublin, where he was responsible for the construction of major waterworks.

Ted Ruddock's edition of William Mylne's letters provides us with the context of Mylne's sojourn and fills in the background of a resonant period in colonial history. The context is important, but the main value of the letters themselves is the detail they provide of an individual's experiences and observations. Mylne was an outsider struggling to prove himself in unfamiliar and demanding surroundings. His is not the only account of Scottish settler experience, but its illumination of a specific time and place is revealing.

Mylne appears not to be sympathetic to the American bid for independence, but it was of great interest to many Scots, and Scottish newspapers and journals contained reports of developments. After independence, there was a surge of migration from Scotland to the United States. Although much of it was not by choice, a key attraction was the promise of political and religious freedom.

Since the publication in 1993 of Mylne's letters there has been a growing interest in Scottish emigration to the United States and the impact of Scots and ideas originating in Scotland in the colonial and postcolonial periods. Mylne himself made little impact. His brief sojourn at Stephen's Creek left little trace, although, as Ruddock outlines, he was on the margins of important developments in the extension of settlement in Georgia. Most of the descriptions of Scottish settler experience, in letters, journals, and published accounts, date from the postcolonial period. The National Library of Scotland holds a substantial collection of this material. The collection includes accounts of dire experiences of hardship and struggle and other accounts that extol the advantages of American opportunity, perhaps above all the chance of owning land, which in Scotland was beyond the imagination of the vast majority. Even for a professional man such as Mylne the ambition to purchase land would have been unrealistic in Scotland. Numerous guides for emigrants were published in the nineteenth century, as well as official British government information, and a growing body of published material draws on these sources.

Mylne's letters illuminate a specific time and place in American colonial history. Alongside research on the experiences and contributions of Scots in the United States, it is interesting to look at the effects of American experiences and ideas on life in Scotland. Mylne's later career was a success. We do not know how much this might be attributed to what he learned from his American sojourn, but it would be interesting to investigate and explore the subsequent lives of other Scottish sojourners and the consequences in their homeland of their American experiences.

JENNI CALDER

## Preface

The five chapters of this book contain a narrative of two years that William Mylne spent in America, from his own pen in letters to his sister Anne and brother Robert. The letters are accompanied by a summary of the historic events that were taking place around Mylne in the southern colonies and by sketches of his earlier life in Scotland and continental Europe and of his subsequent years spent in Ireland.

The letters deserve to be read without interruption and so footnotes have been used sparingly, mainly to clarify unusual words and explain textual inconsistencies. Further background information about persons, places, and events mentioned in the text, as well as notes of sources, have been collected in an annotated index. Asterisks in the text mark the first occurrence of words included as entries in the index.

Mylne wrote his letters with an eye to economy of words and paper—and so of postal charges. He used capitals within sentences as well as for first words, and his punctuation is irregular and sometimes obliterated by the document's age. The scripts have been tidied up only just as much as seemed safe against mistakes in meaning but desirable for ease of reading. Most of the paragraph breaks, some sentence breaks, and a number of full stops and commas have been inserted by the editor, but no changes have been made in any of the writers' spelling or word order. The word *sic* has been used only where the original is otherwise likely to be thought a printer's or editor's muddle. A modern convention has been applied in the use of capitals.

The chance finding of the letters has led me into unexpected areas of research and most interesting travel in the southern states, and also to pleasurable visits to members of the Mylne family over a long period of years. I am most grateful to the Mylnes, initially to Miss Jean Mylne of Great Amwell, who first showed me the letters more than fifteen years ago, and later to Captain W. R. J. Mylne and his family, who have permitted me to continue the study and to publish the letters, some of which were deposited many years ago at the Scottish Record Office in Edinburgh and the remainder placed recently in the British Architectural Library in London. My thanks are also due to the staffs of those archives for their help.

In the United States in 1980 I was received and assisted by all the libraries and archives named in the list of main sources and the index. Particularly helpful were conversations with Heard Robertson and Ray Rowland in Augusta, John Hemphill in Williamsburg, and Edward C. Papenfuse in Annapolis. My base for work in Washington, including the Library of Congress, was the Smithsonian Institution, Division of Mechanical and Civil Engineering, by invitation of the curator, Robert Vogel. The travel and research was supported by a grant from the Leverhulme Trust Fund.

## Chapter 1

## INTRODUCTION: BACKGROUND TO THE JOURNEYS

Six letters written by William Mylne* during a journey to the British colonies in America in 1773-75 form the core of this book. Mylne was an architect and master mason in the city of Edinburgh* and heir to a family tradition nearly three centuries old. About 1481 John Mylne received a grant of the office of "master mason" to King James III of Scotland. Alexander, Thomas, John II, John III, John IV, and finally Robert Mylne (1633-1710)* all held similar appointments to successive kings and queens of Scotland before the office was abolished at the union of the Scottish and English parliaments in 1707. During the years 1671-79 Robert was responsible for the rebuilding, under the architect Sir William Bruce,* of Holyrood Palace, the official residence in Scotland of the British monarchs. William Mylne was a paternal great-grandson of this Robert Mylne. William Mylne's grandfather and father were both prominent masons in Edinburgh at the time when the title "master mason" was ceasing to be synonymous with "architect." Like other masons, William's father, Thomas, wished to provide his two sons with the opportunity to become architects in the new sense of professional designer of buildings and to do so sent them abroad to study. William traveled in France and Italy from 1754 to 1758, and his elder brother, Robert (1733-1811),* joined him at the end of 1754 in Paris and remained in Rome until 1759.

On his return to Edinburgh, William set himself up in business as a mason and general builder, but he was also willing, as an architect, to provide designs for buildings whether or not he contracted

# GENEALOGY OF MYLNES

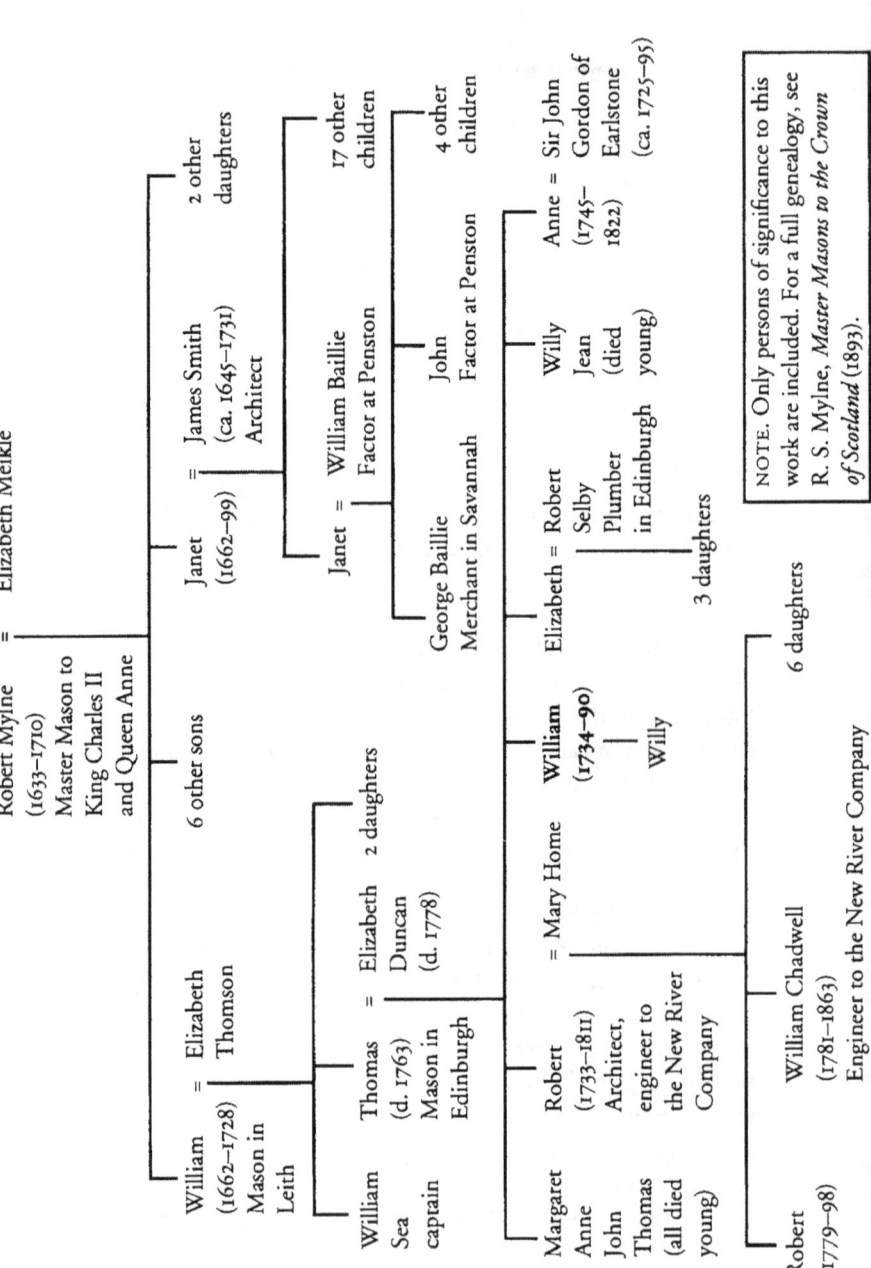

NOTE. Only persons of significance to this work are included. For a full genealogy, see R. S. Mylne, *Master Masons to the Crown of Scotland* (1893).

to build them. He obtained a reasonable quantity of both types of work in Edinburgh and elsewhere in southern Scotland. Robert returned from the Continent with much greater éclat, having won the annual architectural competition of the Academy of Saint Luke at Rome in 1758. He paused in London* in the summer of 1759 to submit a design for the new Blackfriars Bridge* and in February 1760 was appointed its "surveyor," with responsibility for design and for direction of the various contractors as agent for the City of London. He thereupon established his practice as an architect in London; he was soon recognized as a leading member of the profession, obtained important commissions, and became financially successful. The family's traditional mantle of mason and builder in Scotland fell on William.

On several occasions in the next ten years when Robert was approached by clients in Scotland he introduced William to them as architect or as building contractor. He was also able to provide loans or financial guarantees to assist his brother. This ability, with his own success and his status of firstborn (surviving) son, gave him authority in the family that he seems to have overused and that was resented, at least by William and his sister Anne.*

When William returned from Europe, a spirit of enterprise was alive in Scotland, and Edinburgh, the capital, was set to grow. The city would have to break out of its very crowded site on a steep-sided ridge that stretched eastward from the high Castle Rock to Holyrood Palace, with High Street running downhill and connecting the two along the gently sloping spine of the ridge. The town council had already bought land on a parallel but wider ridge to the north, which was separated from the old town by the Nor' Loch, an expanse of shallow and dirty water lying in the hollow between the two. A fine extension of the city could be built on the northern ridge with a bridge across the Nor' Loch to connect it to the old town. Just a year after William's return he was asked by George Drummond,* the current lord provost of Edinburgh and prime mover of the extension, to design a new "north passage" to the old town, which presumably meant a bridge across the Loch. But the project was not pursued, and for some years William had to be content with simpler work, though he became recognized as one of Edinburgh's leading builders. In 1765 the bridge proposal was revived, and William won a contract to build it to his own

Portrait of William Mylne, probably painted after his return from the Continent in 1758. Courtesy of Captain W. R. J. Mylne.

design in an agreed period of four years. It became known as the North Bridge.* Building the bridge gave William more publicity, and other work came his way, though not in floods, perhaps because he was never a man of great ambition. In 1767 a plan was agreed for Edinburgh's "New Town" north of the bridge, and a spate of new building began, and continued for several decades.

Scotland's increasing prosperity was founded on improvements in agriculture and on growing external trade fed internally by increasing manufactures; but to individual Scotsmen these developments brought poverty or depression as often as wealth, and many decided to seek their fortunes abroad. The stimuli for this emigration ranged from high ambition to sheer desperation. While the growth of empire required agents of government and soldiers to serve overseas, and the empire and its trade opened the way for merchants, artisans, and farmers, and also doctors, lawyers, and other professionals to establish their homes and profitable businesses abroad, the social and economic changes in Scotland itself following the "Forty-Five,"* especially in the highlands and islands, brought new depths of poverty to peasant farmers and a first real experience of it to their immediate superiors, the "tacksmen," the first tenants of the land, which they sublet in smaller lots to the peasants. Both were losing their traditional way of life under the impact of "improved" agriculture, which usually involved a reduction of manpower and increase in rents. Their relationship with the landlords was becoming strictly commercial, instead of the former loyalty that had bound them to chief and clan, both for society and mutual protection. A further unsettling influence were the often glowing recommendations of life in America from kinsmen who had already settled there. A steady outflow of Scots had been occurring since the early years of the century; it accelerated after the end of the Seven Years' War in 1763; and in the early 1770s, from the highlands and islands in particular, it became a flood. Many tacksmen were accompanied in emigration by their tenants, and the numbers departing are believed to have reached 1200 in the year 1770 from all the highlands and islands, 870 in 1771 from the islands of Skye* and Islay* only, and more than 1300 from all districts in 1773.

During this frenzy of departures from Scottish ports, William Mylne also left Edinburgh for America, but he left furtively and alone. He went first to London, took lodgings at an undisclosed address and booked a passage on a ship that sailed regularly with cargo to Charleston,* South Carolina.

From there he soon moved to the backcountry at the boundary of the neighboring province of Georgia, where a new phase of white settlement was beginning, with almost all the new settlers coming not from Britain but from the other colonies, especially North and South Carolina. The desire of the governor of Georgia, Sir James Wright,* to extend the settled area of Georgia westward, increasing the white population and the colony's agricultural production, and placing more settled land between the older plantations near the coast and the Indian tribes' hunting grounds, had coincided neatly with a need to help the tribes out of heavy debts to white traders. By a treaty with the Creek* and Cherokee* nations he had relieved them of the debts in exchange for about two million acres of their traditional lands. The traders' accounts were to be settled by the government out of the money paid by new settlers for their grants of land.

William traveled in these "Ceded Lands"* with the holders of the largest grants, but all the agreements soon broke down with the onset of the American Revolution. William had arrived at Charleston on a ship full, or more than half full, of tea; and in the month of his arrival Boston's Sons of Liberty* held their famous Tea Party,* tipping the cargoes of three tea ships into Boston* Harbor to show their determination not to be taxed by the British Parliament, in which they had no representation. The Tea Party moved the British government and its thirteen American colonies a long step nearer to the bitter conflict that ended with the colonies' victory and independence ten years later.

The earlier attempts of the London government to raise revenue in the colonies had met with firm and effective resistance, resulting in 1766 in the repeal of the Stamp Act and in 1770 the rescinding of virtually all the Townshend duties (the tea tax being a notable exception) imposed in 1767.

The King and his prime minister, Lord North,* had two aims in maintaining the tax on tea. One was to ease the financial problems of the East India Company.* Although ostensibly a private company engaged in trade with countries in the East, the East India Company fulfilled all the functions of government in the British possessions and dependencies in Asia and the Pacific. In return both government and Parliament had been happy to give the company a monopoly of trade to the East; but by 1773 it was asking for financial assistance to maintain its trading and quasi-governmental functions, while continuing to pay dividends to its shareholders, who included many of the richest and most influential men in Great Britain.

One of various devices proposed for improving the company's trading balance was a change in the way of selling East India tea in the colonies. Hitherto it had been shipped from the East and landed in London, where a duty was paid; it was then auctioned to merchants who shipped it again to American ports, where a further duty of threepence per pound was levied for the British government. Although some tea reached the colonies thus and the contentious threepence was paid, cheaper tea in much larger quantity was bought by the colonists from Dutch and Danish smugglers. The East India Company thought that by shipping its tea directly to the colonies it could sell it below the price of smuggled tea and so greatly increase its sales.

Parliament agreed to abolish the rule that tea must be landed and sold in London and the duty paid there. But Lord North refused to abolish the duty payable in American ports, attributing his decision to the King himself when he remarked "The King will have it so. The King means to try the question with America." This was their second aim, and it backfired. Though North's remark cannot have been widely known in the colonies at the time, "trying the question" was exactly what vigilant Americans saw as the purpose of the Tea Act\*; and after the act was passed without even a vote at Westminster on May 10, 1773, a chorus of alarm arose in the late summer and fall at protest meetings in Boston and other colonial cities. In London at the same time the arrangements for shipping large quantities of tea went ahead, and William Mylne's departure coincided exactly with their dispatch.

William Mylne's reason for making the journey to America lies in the story of his building of the Edinburgh bridge. It was a large structure for its time, particularly high and therefore heavy on its foundations. William contracted in 1765 to build it for a fixed sum of £10,140, binding himself to put right any failure within its first ten years that was "applicable to the fault of the execution, or of the foundations." His brother Robert and a family friend named Alexander Brown,* a merchant in Edinburgh, were his "cautioners" (or guarantors) in the contract. As William was building the bridge he discovered that it needed deeper and wider foundations than he had allowed for in the contract sum; and various parts of the side walls also had to be thickened. Although his profit would be reduced by these changes, he asked no extra payment and almost completed the bridge before the date agreed. Then disaster struck. At half-past eight o'clock on the evening of August 3, 1769, when members of the public were walking on the unfinished roadway of the bridge, a large section of the south approach suddenly crumbled. Masonry vaults inside it collapsed, one side wall fell outward, and the mass of earthfill over the vaults subsided, engulfing five people, whose bodies took many days to recover.

Of the immediate effect on William there is no record; of the subsequent investigations to establish the cause of failure and the arguments about responsibility and methods of repair, there is almost a surfeit. William was required to take down large parts of the bridge that had not failed, in order to ascertain by inspection whether they were safe, and then to rebuild them. He was only bound by contract to rebuild at his own expense those parts that were found to be wrongly built or inadequately founded, but he had to borrow a lot of money to pay for the work because much of the money that would become due to him was withheld, awaiting the consideration of the appointed arbiter, a senior judge named Lord Elliock.* William's largest creditor was Robert, from whom he started borrowing immediately after the accident. By September 1772 this debt amounted to £1,671, and he had also borrowed from other members of his family and friends. The strain on him was long and undoubtedly severe. He became ill, though unfortunately the nature of this clearly recurrent sickness is not recorded. That his normal place of residence was a house in Halkerstone's Wynd,* standing quite literally in the shadow of the south approach of the bridge, can only have deepened his depression. He eventually felt persecuted by the town council, as they demanded investigation by demolition of more and more parts of the bridge, and was deeply embarrassed by his debt to Robert, the proud brother on whom he had become so dependent.

In September 1772 the reconstruction was virtually finished and the arbiter recommended the council to make some payment to help William out of his debts. In answer they made him a loan of £1,000, but they then failed to finish metaling the road on the bridge, which was outside William's contract, before the end of the year. In January 1773 public concern was aroused about yet another wall and the council called new inspectors and demanded another round of demolition and rebuilding. This time William failed to answer. He was absent from his house when the city chamberlain delivered an "instrument of protest" on March 26. He contested it in April with his own "instrument of protest" against the council and then fell silent until on May 2 he wrote the brief letter to his mother that opens our next chapter.

The settlement of accounts lay unattended for a long time; but work on the bridge was soon resumed under the council's overseer John Wilson,* though slowly, it seems, for the bridge was not completed until August 1775. In all, the council's extra costs were well over £7,000. Some part of this could only be justified as the cost of allaying fears and reassuring the public; and how much of the repair work done by William Mylne was unnecessary it is now impossible to judge.

## Chapter 2

## BEFORE DEPARTURE

To Mrs Mylne, Pouderhall.*

Dear Mother,*
  As I have now no further occassion for the furniture of the house in Halkerstones wynd which I am now leaving, I beg you will accept of it and likewise any silver work that I am possesd of, as some small compensation for the extroardinary expence you have been at on my account.

I am,
  Dear mother,
    Your ever affectionate son
      Willm. Mylne.
Edin$^r$ 2$^{nd}$ May 1773.

---

William's whereabouts for the next three and a half months are unknown. His baggage was carried to London on board the *Betsie* (or *Betsey*), which sailed from Leith* on August 17.

After the Tea Act was passed by Parliament on May 10, the East India Company began making arrangements to ship its first consignments to American ports. The company decided to select a small number of well-known importers in each of the major colonial ports, Boston, New York,* Philadelphia* and Charleston, and appoint them agents to receive the tea and sell it on behalf of the company for a commission fixed at six percent. It cannot be doubted that all of these chosen consignees were known to have Tory sympathies; and it was inevitable that any Tory leanings of other merchants in the colonial ports would be weakened or de-

Powderhall in the late nineteenth century.
From J. Grant, *Old and New Edinburgh* (1883), vol. 3, p. 93.

stroyed by their exclusion from the new tea trade. The company had simply chosen an easy way of marketing the tea with assured profit, ignoring any risk of a political reaction. The names of the consignees were announced in London on August 4; but because communication with them in America took many weeks, they themselves only learned of their involvement when their consignments were in mid-Atlantic or nearing the American ports, and in those ports there was a rising storm of opposition to the new tea imports.

The arrangements for shipping the tea began as soon as the consignees' names were announced. Immediate deposits of one-eighth of the value of consignments were made in London by the agents or underwriters for the consignees, full payment being required two months after arrival of the cargoes in American ports. The import duty at destination was to be paid by the consignees, but with bills of exchange drawn on the East India Company, which meant that payment of the duty would actually be made to the Treasury by the company in London.

The vessels chosen to carry the tea were the *Eleanor,* the *Dartmouth* and the *Beaver* all bound for Boston, the *Polly* for Philadelphia, the *Nancy* for New York, and the *London* for Charleston. The shipments totalled two thousand chests of tea, each containing 320 pounds, of which two hundred and fifty-seven chests were bound for Charleston on the *London*.

---

Dear Nany,[1]                                              29$^{th}$ August 1773.

    I have received from the mate of the *Betsey* my trunk, box, & gun, all in good order, it was only last Friday, and I began to be uneasy about them. When at the wharf, I heard one of the clerks say there was a cask for a Mr Mylne also, the mate answered that was for Rob$^t$ Mylne Esq$^{re}$ Architect, you may guess where it comes from.[2] The same morning after I had got my things to my lodging and was going out again, who should I see coming down the street but his honour.[3] At first I suspected he was in search of me, I stept asside, and observed he past our door, I was very glad of it, for although in my present temper of mind I should have paid little regard to him, he still had it in his power to have embarrassed me very much in my intended voyage; I pray to God we don't meet, for it must be very disagreeable to both of us. I hope it will not happen as I have but a few days longer to remain here, for on Saturday I took my passage on board the *London,* Cap$^{tn}$ Curling,* bound for Charles Town South Carolina, who sails the end of this week, and the cap$^n$ desires my things may be in the ship by Thursday; and to show you how good a economist I am turned, and how little I regard appearances, I must inform you how I managed this matter. I went to the Carolina coffee house where I found bills hung up for several vessels going to Carolina. I asked if any of the Capt$^{ns}$ were in the room. A Capt$^n$ Wilson* was pointed out to me, I went to him he said the passage was ten guineas, and to find myself in provisions, that the passengers always met and agreed among themselves what to lay in, which he provided for

---

1. William's common name for his sister Anne.
2. Robert relished his wine. The cask may have been ordered from Alexander Brown.
3. William's frequent mode of reference to Robert.

Engraving of Robert Mylne,
from a miniature painted by his daughter Maria.

them—receiving money for that purpose; that the provisions and drink generally, at the lowest, cost fifteen guineas, which made the whole come to twenty five guineas, this was the expence of a cabbin passenger.

I was a good deal surprised to find I had been so far out in my calculation, which was oweing to the books I have lately read. When I came home, I laid my plan, and next morning got a boat and went aboard Capt$^n$ Curling's ship, luckely he came at the same time, I told him I wanted to go as a steerage passenger, and to know the terms and accomodation I could have, he told me the passage was eight guineas, that I should be furnished with ships provisions, that if I chused tea or coffee I must buy them myself, that I would sleep in a hammock, and that I must bring my own bedding. I immediatly agreed with him, this now brings my expence within what I had proposed at setting out, and enables me to purchase several little necessaries I might have occassion for, that otherwise I must have gone without, at the same time preserves the capital I proposed to have on my arrival. The *London* is a fine large ship, very clean and airy, the capt$^n$ a young sedate man, about thirty, very civil and sensible as far as I could judge, I think I shall be full as easy as if I had gone a cabbin passenger; from what I had seen aboard the collier[4] I know the ships provisions are of the very best kind, you know I can do with anything and they must be bad indeed if I cannot put up with them. I beged the capt$^n$ would be so good to allow one of his people to assist me in buying my bedding; he directly desired one of the mates to go along with me for this purpose whenever I pleased, and likewise that he should do me any other service I might have occassion for.

Last night in stepping into a shop to sell my bad guinea, I lost Mungo.*[5] It was at the Exchange* and about a mile from where I lodge, I was very uneasy, I could not think of losing him when he had stuck so close to me, I went in search of him which after some time I was obliged to give up. I then went to the coffee house I frequent, thinking he might have gone there, and then home, and when the door opened, bounce came Mungo up to my very throat. I understood he had come directly to the house and had

---

4. Presumably a ship on which he had traveled from Leith to London.
5. William Mylne's dog, who accompanied him from Edinburgh.

been there some time. It is very surprising how the creature could find his way through the turnings and streets and so many people in so short a time. As I am never able to eat one third of what is set before me Mungo fares well, but within these two days he is turned as delicate as his master and will eat nothing but lean.

Yesterday I met Jock Learmont* gayley dressed, we passed close to one another, he did not know me. I don't in any manner confine myself, but the limits have been as yet towards the West End* of the town—no farther than Saint Pauls.* I have wrote this far on Sunday.

Saturday the 4$^{th}$ Sept$^{r.}$

I thought before this to have been at sea but something has happened that delays the ships sailing till next week, the capt$^n$ says Wednesday next. There are four ships going together, so we shall have company, unless seperated, all the way. I wish now I had not by my last confined your writing to the first post, as I might at least have heard your intelligence ex$^{dy}$ from P——d——ll.$^6$ I begin to be quite tired of London—although I walk out in the country some miles every day. Last night I happened to stroll into Moorfields* at one end of which stands an hospitall; I enquired how it was called, it was Bedlam;* instantly the Man of Feeling's story rushed on my mind, I left the place, I am as chicken-hearted as ever.

I have given over buying, having laid out three or four pounds more than I at first intended, that I might have no wish unsatisfied, and my situation may be easier where I am going. My way of life at present is, breakfast at 8, walk out till 2, dines, sit an hour, come home and read, walk out till near dark, go to the Bear house,$^7$ sup one night, one two penny worth of oysters, the other on cucumbers, 3 a halfpenny, a pint of beer. My dinner is extravagant being 14 or 15 pence.

I see by the newspapers there are 400 highlanders going to Carolina, I suppose that part of your country will be a desart soon.

---

6. ". . . intelligence extraordinary from Powderhall."
7. A public house or hostelry. "Bear" or "bere" was the name of a type of barley, but the term died out, first in the south and later in the north of England and Scotland.

I have got a new coat of a forrest cloath, 2 pair of breeches, a hat, 2 pair of shoes, 4 check shirts, 6 pair stockings, 4 handkerchiefs, I have bought some books, fishing tackle of all kinds, pouder & shot and a number of other little things which obliged me to add a packing box to my other luggage. They are all shipt on board the *London* and I have likewise paid my passage.

I should imagine it was oweing to the Selby's* you was not inabled to write by the first post, I wish it had been otherwise, for now I cannot hear from you till long after my arrivall in Carolina. I had a good prospect of settling in this place, the Bear house I frequent is kept by a widow of thirty six, has been well looked, she for what reason has taken a fancy to me, she first began the attack on Mungo of whom she grew very fond, she carried it on by degrees till at last I have left the house. She thought I was a good natured man, could count and write. I might have done worse however, the house is well frequented, the pots all silver—how would you have liked me selling a tankard of beer?

This day I took a long stroll, I found myself near Islington;* thought I, if his honour is at the Water works and we meet, there will be a fine piece of work. It came on rain and I was obliged to house, I asked if a beef stake was to be had, no such thing, they were fine salmon at the door, I got a plate and bought a groats[8] worth, which was sufficient for dinner, it was pickled, I am surprised how they could sell it so cheap, it was as much as I could eat.

This town is much altered to the advantage since I was here before, the minories* which lately there was no crossing is now better paved than the high street of Edin$^r$, as are all the streets in Wapping,* which I remember a pudle. Last Sunday afternoon I took a long walk on the Surry side and came over Blackfriars Bridge. To give the devil his due[9] it is a noble piece of work, the avenues are so compleat on that side, nothing can be better done, when those on the London side are finished it will far eclipse Westminster Bridge.*

I forgot to mention my bed, it consists of a matress and pillow,

---

8. A groat was worth four pence.
9. Mylne refers here to his brother Robert, architect of Blackfriars Bridge.

a blanket and a covering, I believe I must add another blanket. They are all clean and neat, very cheap and will be of service to me in America. Although I am impatient to be gone yet my mind enjoyes that peace inwardly to which it has been so long a stranger. Here there is little enjoyment without entering into the greater or smaller circles, my walk is without them. Poverty & extravagence, folly & vice are strangely blended together, if your ears are dea'ved with the cries of the beggar, your eyes are saluted at the same time with the most pompous equipages, & last night Lady Huntingtons* preacher was holding furth at one end of Tower Hill* to a crowded audience, among which were many coaches and chaises, while a foreign quack doctor was luring the blind and the lame at the other; in the middle space the mob were entertaining themselves with ducking a poor wretch who had picked a man's pocket, one of the doctor's audience, in the Tower Ditch and half drowned him.

After long revolving in my own mind in what manner I should setle the management of my affairs, I have at last come to the resolution of sending a power of attorney to Livingston* to act. This I can recall when I please, I will send it to my brother along with the letter I shall write to him at the moment the ship is under sail; leaving it in his power to forward or not as he thinks proper. In my letter to our brother I shall let him know that my intention was to have divested myself of all my effects in his favour for the behoof of my creditors, but this could not be done without papers and the rights of process. I shall let him know that as soon as I arrive at my port I will write, when the form of a paper may be sent over in any shape he pleases, which I shall execute. After long thinking this occurred to me the best conclusion I could come to, I have employed an attorney for this purpose. I shall write you a few lines before I go and along with them shall send my will properly done and witnessed. I send this away that you may not think any accident has happened to me.

My duty to our mother, my best respects to the Selby family in case my secret has transpired, but I desire it may always be given out that I am gone for health, which will be a reason when I write to his honour. I shall not write Livingston on this occassion. If you receive any money or pay on my acc$^t$ set it down distinctly in case his honour should come to have a finger in the pye—take good care of the money I left with you for your own sake, put it into Mansfields* hands in your name.

I think as soon as I get a setlement to bring Willy*  [10] over— I can learn him any part of education that is necessary for him. Believe me to be your ever affectionate brother

Will<sup>m</sup> Mylne

The weather has been very hot here ever since I came till this day when it has rained much.

---

10. William Mylne's illegitimate son.

## Chapter 3

## SOUTH CAROLINA
## AND GEORGIA

The *London* sailed down the Thames on September 19 with the *Elizabeth*, the *Carolina Packet*, and the *Good Intent*, all bound for Carolina. At Deal they stopped to await a favorable wind, as it was then blowing from the southwest up the English Channel. They lay there for ten days, being joined during the time by other ships, including the tea ships *Polly* for Philadelphia and *Dartmouth* for Boston. On September 29 they all sailed for America. When the *London* berthed in Charleston Harbor on Thursday, December 2 it is probable that William Mylne went immediately to lodge with John Hatfield,* merchant, in King Street. He mentioned in a later letter that he suffered "a severe fit of sickness" at Charleston, which may explain his surprising silence about events that followed the arrival of the *London*. Alternative reasons can be suggested, such as unwillingness to cause concern in the minds of his relatives at home or deliberate avoidance of public controversy. It is even more likely that he dealt with his time at Charleston in a letter that has not survived.

The people of Charleston could not fail to take note of the *London*'s arrival and its cargo of tea. Charleston was the hub and main seaport of a huge territory of rich agriculture, including all of South Carolina, part of Georgia, and a large proportion of North Carolina. Its mercantile and shipping business handled the export of rice, indigo, other crops, and skins from this large area and also satisfied the planters' needs for imported equipment, special materials, and most important, slaves. The rich men of Charleston were mainly merchants and planters, both heavily dependent for their prosperity on external trade. Despite this they had agreed to and operated, together with a third group, the artisans or "mechanics," an effective embargo on importation of British goods in 1769. The mechanics had everything to gain by the ban on British manufactured goods, which competed with their own products, but they had also established themselves as the loudest exponents of political radicalism in the city—except, perhaps, for Peter Timothy,* the editor of Charleston's weekly newspaper, the *South Carolina Gazette*.

The *Gazette* alerted its readers on November 15 to the approach of a cargo of tea; on the twenty-second it named the ship as the *London* and proposed a voluntary pledge by all merchants not to accept the East India Company's tea while the threepence duty remained in force. On December 6 and in subsequent issues it reported the *London*'s arrival and the events that followed, always accompanied by strongly anti-British comment and news of resistance in Boston, Philadelphia, and New York.

On December 3, the day after the *London*'s arrival, all the city's inhabitants were called to a meeting in the Great Hall over the Exchange, where the consignees of the tea, Roger Smith, Esq., and Messrs. Leger and Greenwood, publicly renounced their interest in the cargo to loud applause. An agreement not to import any more tea subject to the duty was signed by several merchants at the meeting and by more than fifty others on the following day. Captain Curling was roundly told at the meeting to take his cargo back to England.

Opinion in Charleston, however, was not unanimous, and the *London* continued to lie at the wharf. The separate groups of the populace were considering their attitudes, and on Wednesday, December 15 the planters and landholders first, and later the mechanics, held separate meetings at Mrs. Swallow's Tavern—Mrs. Swallow was, almost certainly, John Hatfield's mother-in-law. On the following day a "merchants' committee" met at her tavern. On December 17 there was a second meeting for all inhabitants at the Exchange, lasting for five hours; there it emerged that a number of merchants (said to be "very few" by the *Gazette*), having previously imported tea in modest quantities and paid the duty, did not see the need to give up their trade for a new political stand against the principle of taxation without representation. The previous resolutions were confirmed, but not unanimously, and it was necessary to decide that there should be another general meeting in January. Both parties were, of course, unaware that the Boston "mob" had, on the previous day, held a "tea party" that would soon bring political developments into daily confusion with the conduct of all their businesses.

The Charleston collector of customs and the lieutenant-governor of South Carolina, William Bull,* were watching these developments. It has been said that Bull received reports of threats of violence on Captain Curling. The law required the collector, when the cargo had been twenty days in port without its duty paid, to land it and lodge it in a "King's warehouse." On the morning of December 22 he therefore took action. As the *Gazette* reported

> Very early, the hoisting out of the ship's hold, delivery to the King's officers, and landing by the Collector, was begun; and the whole two hundred and fifty-seven chests were put on shore, carried up in drays, stowed away, and locked up, in a cellar under the Exchange, hired for that purpose, with so much expedition, that the whole was completed, by the time that the people in general imagined it would be begun; indeed, there never was an instance here, of so great a number of packages, being taken out of any vessel, and thus disposed of, in so short a time. The Sheriff, and other peace officers, we hear, had particular instructions given to them, in case there should appear a disposition to obstruct the landing of the tea by the Collector, in any way that could be deemed a breach of the peace; but the people, though not pleased with seeing it landed at all, were perfectly quiet; as they did, upon the tea being taken into the charge of the Collector, and do still, confidently rely, upon its remaining locked up, in the cellar where it is now lodged, until orders may arrive, after the East India Company shall have received advice of its present disposition, to reship it for England; or until, by a proper attention to their interest, and an exertion of their influence, they shall have prevailed upon Parliament to repeal the impolitic and offensive duty. . . .

Captain Curling's cargo of tea lay in the cellar for nearly three years. It was joined by several small consignments landed during 1774 and not accepted by any merchant. In November 1774 there arrived seven casks that had been loaded in London without the knowledge of the ship's master and which the consignees emptied patriotically into the harbor, a Charleston Tea Party. The tea in the cellar remained there until October 1776, when it was taken out and sold for the benefit of the new state of South Carolina, reportedly for a good price.

Of William Mylne's experience of the voyage and arrival of the tea we know only that he was there. He left Charleston for the backlands probably before the middle of January, stopped for some time at Augusta,* on the Georgia side of the Savannah River,* then before the end of February moved back across the river to occupy a log cabin in the woods by Stephen's Creek,* about seven miles up the Savannah from Augusta.

Augusta stands about one hundred and fifty miles up the Savannah River on the south (or southwestern) side. It is less than three miles downstream from the rapids that, in the late eighteenth century, formed a stop to navigation, as the river fell over the rim of the rocks of the piedmont terrain into the great coastal plain of eastern North America.

The meeting of several ancient overland trails, adjacent to easy river crossings, had for a long time made it a place of strategic importance. A group of Indians called the Savannahs had set up their "town" there in the 1680s, giving their name to the river. The land on both sides of the river fell within the territory granted to South Carolina by King Charles II's charter in 1663, and the Carolinians carried on a busy trade, as well as intermittent warfare, with the Indians of the region, buying deer and beaver skins and selling manufactured goods including firearms. But when King George II created the new province of Georgia by charter in 1732 he gave all rights to land and trade south of the Savannah River to the trustees of the new province. It was to be a high-minded colony in which both slavery and the sale of rum were prohibited. The trustees' representative, General James Oglethorpe,* arrived in the Savannah River with a party of 115 colonists early in the following year and began to build the city which was also called Savannah.*

An Act of Parliament passed in London in 1735 ruled that trade with the Indians on the south side of the river—in the Georgia backlands—could only be undertaken by traders licensed in Georgia, and Oglethorpe's officers began immediately to harrass Carolinian traders who were not so licensed. He also planned a new white township on the south side of the river to supersede the trading town called New Windsor that had grown around the

Carolinians' garrison at Fort Moore* on the north bank. The new town would be three miles further upstream and would be called Augusta after the Princess of Wales.

The transfer of business took place very quickly, in spite of Carolinian dissent. After only five years six hundred traders were operating through Augusta, and very little trade remained at New Windsor. Augusta's economic buoyancy continued throughout the colonial era, the merchants and chief traders earning the sobriquet "gentlemen of Augusta," with their confidence and life-style resembling somewhat those of the long-established Charleston merchant class.

Augusta was laid out with a church, called Saint Paul's, a fort, and a grid plan of forty lots, each of one acre. With land grants of up to five hundred acres available outside the town, however, some merchants built their houses and stores beyond the grid. In the eyes of a British colonel in 1779, Augusta was "a number of straggling houses, arranged in a long street lying parallel to the river; at the distance of 100 yards." The fort built on the edge of the central grid would house a garrison and stores of weapons and ammunition but could not protect the more distant buildings, even if it were in good condition. In fact it fell quickly into disrepair, being built of wood with the puncheons (halved trees forming the vertical posts of the stockade) driven into the ground and subject to rapid decay.

The trustees' charter was surrendered in 1752 and Georgia became a colonial province vested in the Crown. Slavery was legalized but the ban on rum remained. In 1758 it was divided into seven parishes for administrative purposes, the "frontier" parish to the northwest being Saint Paul's Parish* centered on Augusta, but with no clear western boundary to show where white settlement should end and Indian hunting ground begin. After the end of the Seven Years' War in 1763, during which only the Cherokee had taken up arms against the British, boundaries were agreed upon at a major conference in Augusta between the governors of the four southern colonies and representatives, numbering fully eight hundred men, of the five tribes: Chickasaw,* Choctaw,* Creek, Cherokee, and Catawba. Also present was the king's newly appointed superintendent of Indian affairs in the South, John Stuart,* a man of great influence among the Indians. The boundaries of Saint Paul's Parish to the northwest and southwest were set on the lines of the Little River* and the Ogeechee River,* which meant a considerable loss of territory for the Creeks. Though agreed upon in 1763, the boundaries were not clearly marked out on the ground until 1768.

By contemporary proclamation made in London in October 1763, the British government confirmed the Indians' right to all the lands reserved to them by previous agreements, denied any right of white settlement in those lands, and reserved all rights of purchase of such territory to governors or commander-in-chief only, on behalf of the Crown. All land west of the boundaries agreed at the Augusta conference became subject to these strictures. By the same proclamation the right of trading with the Indians was opened up to white men holding licenses issued by any of the southern governors, thus breaking the virtual monopoly of the Indian trade that the Augusta merchants had exercised with the support of two successive governors of Georgia. Most of these "gentlemen of Augusta" never traveled to the Indian settlements where the actual trading took place but supplied the men who did so. Some merchants paid traders as their own regular employees. The 1763 agreement also guaranteed the Indians the use of their ancient paths and freedom to visit Augusta and its gentlemen.

From 1757 onward a few white men had been encouraged by the provincial government to settle beyond the agreed boundaries, all on land near the Savannah, Broad,* and Little rivers. This was rich land for cultivation and after 1763 more whites who were already hardened to frontier conditions in provinces further north arrived to become settlers within the new boundaries, and some to be illegal "squatters" beyond them. Most of these people were unsympathetic to the Indians and afraid of them, an attitude quite different from that of the traders newly licensed under the terms of the proclamation. The traders needed friendship and good communication with the Indians, but were in practice too ready to cheat them or bribe them with rum, and after such events, angry Indians were apt to take vengeance on the settlers instead of the traders.

For the seven years that followed the treaty and proclamation of 1763, Augusta remained prosperous and its population increased, but resentments and sporadic incidents of violence occurred. John Stuart's "superintendence" of Indian affairs certainly became more difficult, and its success more problematic as the backlands filled up with new settlers and traders.

William Mylne, in his cabin by Stephen's Creek, was within the influence of Augusta, but was not in Georgia. The South Carolina boundary of white settlement demarcated in 1766 was at least forty miles further up the Savannah than the boundary at Little River on the Georgia side; and the white population on that side was thinly spread on separate plantations. Though Mylne's next surviving letter, to his sister, was dispatched from Augusta, it was clearly written at his cabin.

---

Augusta 29<sup>th</sup> May 1774

Would you believe that in this southern climate My Dearest Nanny we have had so sharp a frost that the trees had the same appearance as in the end of October, the leaves fell, as at the approach of winter, it happened on the 5<sup>th</sup> of this month. I had planted a small garden, in which I had sowen seeds of different kinds. My cucumbers, water & musk melons, and several other vegetables were destroyed, my orchard of peaches which I mentioned in my last, is almost quite destroyed, the country in general has suffered greatly, the wheat which had a fine appearance is in some places wholly ruined, in others on[e] half. The Indian corn that was above ground was bit closs to the surface, however they say this will come forward; it is so far lucky, as the greatest part of their bread is made of this grain. I was a few days ago in a field of indigo, one fourth of it was killed, it was of the wild kind which had been planted before winter. The night was so cold, that although I had a blanket and worsted cover upon me I was obliged to rise and make a fire. The oldest man that lives in these parts does not remember such a frost at this time of the year.

I have now lived above three months in the woods by myself, I have only been twice in Augusta in all that time, sometimes I am eight–ten days without seeing a human creature. I have had time to think about my situation. My plan of life must be regulate[d] by your letters. A planter's life is that I would prefer. Before I turned so much recluse I have been at pains to enquire the produce and profits, they are great; yet the planters are mostly poor, the reason of this is the great prices they are obliged to pay to the store keepers for cloaths and necessaries for themselves and families. They have no manufacture in the country, the tabbaco they grow goes to England and Scotland and comes out to them again in snuff etc. Hemp and flax the same, unless it is some cotton they plant which their wives and daughters spin and weave, for the men does nothing but minds their plantations and hardly that, if they get as much as puts over the year they care for no more; this is with regard to the original setlers, but there are a set of industrious planters coming fast in from Virginia, North Carolina, Pensilvania, and New England, these bring in with them a good number of negroes, they buy the plantations of the old setlers, yet these are in great want of money, what with the long journey the expence of bringing large families so far, the buying land, and maintenance for some time they are generally in debt to the storekeeper who gives them his own price for their produce and that in goods not in money. Their are few stores in this part, people comes twenty mile, a few of the planters who can afford it send their produce to Charlestown or Savannah by water or land carriage. Yet these new planters in a short time by their industry will be able to live easily the ground is so excellent in these back parts producing much larger crops than lower down.

And now for myself my plan would be to purchase a track of land upon this or some other navigable river, to buy three negroes, to bring Willie and a white maid servant over, with these I could live easily and contented, lay by some money yearly. This would require a capital of betwixt £300 & £400, your letters must inform me whether I have any reason to expect this, or not. If I had any prospect that my personal attendance could bring this sum out of the wreck of my fortune I would come over and after setling my affairs I could bring out what necessaries I might want for the rest of my life. My health thank God is perfectly reestablished, I do not think I ever was so well. Although it now begins to be hot yet I have felt it as hot in Scotland, they tell me it will be warmer still but the mornings and evenings are cool and it lasts but for three months.

I wrote in my last of the 26th of April for you to send me a credit for £50, that I suppose you have done, unless I buy land I shall not use it. The necessaries I shall want in case you are of opinion I can be of no service by coming home are, some linnen wastcoats, such as his honour of London used to wear in summer, two jackets of the same, the one to wash the other, two pair stocking breeches, a scarlet serge wastcoat and jacket, the jacket lappeled, this is for winter, half dozen check shirts, half dozen do. white a little finer than the coarse nightshirt I brought out, some thread stockings, two or three pair of worsted ditto, two pair of shoes, a hat about 12 or 15 shillings price, a blue or grey dufle great coat, I could wish for a blue or black corderoe silk wastcoat to wear with a coat I bought in London, this when I went among the gentles, for at Augusta they dress gayly both men and women, I generally wear a check shirt at the Hermitage. I have been so good a husband of my shirts that of the new dozen I have only had on three, and that but for once.

I could wish to have a small chest of wright's tools,[1] with two saws, the one larger than the other, and if the crosscut saw which I left at home is not sold, send it, I wish to God I had all the trumpery I left [t]here, what a money I could make of it. I was going to say some pounds of Scotch snuff in botles, but I make a shift for I manufacture it by drying the leaf at a fire, then puts it into a piece of leather and beats it with a hammer, till it becomes snuff, necessity is the mother of invention. I shall want two pair more of sheets, two table cloaths, some towels, it was lucky you thought of the sheets that I brought with me. I could wish for a feather bed but that perhaps may be got here, if I turn so lazy as want one. I ly at present on a wool matress laid on planks, and although it is very hard when one thinks how they used to ly, yet I sleep sound.

If £300 or £400 is not expected to be raised out of the ruins of my fortune do not send any of these articles, for I would rather perish than that you should want on my account, and indeed I should have no use for them for I must alter my plan, it is impossible for me to do anything in those woods by myself, there are trees to cut down, roots to grub up, the ground to plow, corn, indigo, tobacco, to plant. At present great part of my time is lost in providing victuals for myself, this I mostly do by my gun and fishing. I catched two large fish tother day each two feet long, if

1. *Wright* was the Scottish term for a carpenter.

I had convenience I would salt them, pray send me a receipt how the[y] cure salmon for kitting,[2] their is fish here of several kinds I am sure would answer.

If you send the things send some books, pamphelets, magazines, anything to read. Let me know who is dead, who is married, and who has miscarried, does the same rascals rule the roast in the Town Council; I want much an artificial little fish for fishing with. Ker* could procure you one; how does he, he is an honest fellow, does the sun shine upon him yet? I am afraid not.

We are still in suspence whether there is to be war or not, a few days ago some Indians came in to Augusta, with white feathers, their symbol of peace, they brought no talk, they wanted to hear one.

Never wait for a letter from me but write at least once a month. There may be some things you can spare and which may be usefull, send them, one pays three prices for every thing they buy, I dare say Ramsay* the taylor has my measures & some of the shoemakers will have that of my foot. Let the things, in case you send them, be directed to the care of Mr John Hatefield, Kings Street, Charlestown, I am within four days ride of that place and propose going down at the beggining of winter which is at the time ships come in. Write me in answer to this two copies one directed to me at Robert Mackay's* Esq$^{re}$, Augusta in Georgia, the other to Mr John Hatefields, Kings Street, Charlestown. I do this that I may be sure of an answer, for everything depends upon it. Do not wait for ships sailing but write by the Post, there is a packet comes once a month.

Duncan Robinson* would be a good hand for manageing the sending of the things, he is concerned in ships that come to Charlestown. I want half dozen of knives and forks and a half dozen of spoons, metal or pewter.

If money could be raised now I would buy the land immediatly, and set about clearing it and get myself setled as fast as I could, perhaps you might come over and pass a summer or two with me, Jock Tomson's wife[3] did so to her brother. You would find a most

---

2. Preserved salmon was packed into small wooden containers called "kits" for transport to London.
3. Unidentified.

delightfull country. In stocking the plantation I can buy a cow calve for thirty six shillings, hogs with pigs for about seven shillings; the cows may be such as would give with you three pound ten shillings or four pounds sterling.

My neighbours are mostly all Babtists, I some times go to their meetings, the young women are generally pretty oweing to the goodness of the climate, the men are stout and well made but are mere indians to their women making them do all the work. On Sundays the lasses are clean and neat, on working days you would hardly know them to be the same. Towards Charlestown and the sea coast the people look all as if risen out of a fit of sickness; here is health and strength, but the men are cursedly lazy, some of them makes their wives plant corn.

The water here is excellent. When I don't eat fish I live on butter, cheese, and eggs; I pay six pence the pound for butter, five pence for cheese, eggs I have of my own, I have two hens sitting, one might raise hundreds of chickens for little, corn is so cheap. I don't eat much flesh. As this is the first year I intend to season myself so that I shall be able to endure the weather without fear afterwards.

I have wrote to Livingston but made no mention of coming home, if you should see him take no notice of that, I must be regulate[d] in that point by you.

*Augusta 8th June*

May God Almighty bless and preserve my dear Mother. My love to the Selby family. Write me soon and often till I desire you to stop. Adieu. Believe me to be My Dearest Nanny your truly affectionate

Will<sup>m</sup> Mylne.

---

*From my hermitage on Stephen's Creek
26th June 1774.*

Dear Bob[4]

I write to you last although I like you better than any of the male creation I left at home—I dare say your good sense will easily

---

4. Robert Mylne.

excuse my coming away without a farewell, these adiew's are painfull to any one, but must have been more so in my situation. I found myself fast a going, my health ruined by having disagreable objects before my eyes and no comfort within my hearing; what could I do at home; nothing; my hands were tied, I was certain if anything could recover me it would be a ramble. Nature formed me for travelling, I believe I am of the Tartar kind—whithout any disparagement to the Mylne's blood that runs in my veins. I travelled at as little expence as any man could do, I learnt this in my younger days, and had it not been for a severe fit of sickness I had at Charlestown, my whole journey hither would have cost less than I used to spend in a London jaunt. I believe it was the last efforts of my disorder with my constitution, the battle ended in a violent flux[5] which had well nigh carried me off, since that time I have enjoyed an uninterrupted state of good health.

    I shall not trouble you with an account of the events that have happened to me in my coming hither, I wrote a kind of an abstract to Nanny which I make no doubt she has communicated to you. I have several friends at Augusta at whose houses and tables I am always welcome; Mr Mackay, one of the principal merchants concerned in the trade with the Indians of those parts, made me an offer of his house to live at, this I declined, wanting to live in a retired manner for some time untill I could settle my mind which had been so long discomposed. In one of my rambles in the month of February last I learnt I might rent the place I now live at. It is situate on Stephen's Creek, the house or cabbin is built of pine trees laid a top of one the other, it is covered with what they call clap boards, these are split pines & hung by pinns on the lath, the contents in the inside sixteen feet by twelve. In the corner stands my bed which is of boards, upon these is a matrass, although it is hard yet I sleep sound. Opposite to this is my chest with a few shirts in it, behind which one of my hens has brought me nine chickens. I have a small gallin pot, a frying pan for cooking, I go to the miln for meal made of indian corn, it is three miles distance, it would make you laugh to see me sitting a horse back on the top of the meal bags. I have a peach orchard in which there was an incredible number of peaches before a frost we had in the month

---

5. Dysentery or bleeding from the bowels.

of May, but still there are many more left than I shall use. I have a small garden cultivate with my own hands, in which are greens of different kinds, cucumbers, musk and water melons. I have cured bacon within the house, butter I have at six pence a pound, cheese at five pence, six hens I have layes me more eggs than I can eat and I am rearing chickens, when I want broth I go to the woods and shoot a squirrel or two, this makes excellent [broth], fish I have in the creek.

I have a good horse (for there is no doing without one), he runs in the woods and obeys my call when I want him, he will come running at a mile's distance when he hears my voice. There is a little bird that has built her nest opposite to my bed that wakens me in the morning by its sprightly notes, its nest I am obliged to guard for fear of a cat that has come to me from the woods, this creature has become very tame, she furs about my legs when I get out of bed, I suppose she belonged to the people who had left the house.

Now says you what do you want—Yes, I do want; God Almighty has planted in our breasts an active principle for wise purposes; I feel this at present in a very strong degree; I want again to be in action now the machine is repaired. I want money to purchase some land, and a few negroes to cultivate it under my directions, and with my assistance. All the best land had been taken up by a set of men who now sell it out to newcomers. The life of a planter is that I should like, in it I could lay by money; I have learnt the methods to cultivate the different articles of produce in this country; betwixt £300 & £400 would set me up & every year I should lay by some money. Be so good as inform your self if this is expected out of the wreck of my fortune, if it is not I must stear some other course. I have lived many years to little purpose; you are no stranger to the vexations I have endured, and the friendly part you acted during them, I shall always have a gratefull remembrance of.

There is a tract of land of 300 acres fin[e]ly situate on the River Savannah, this place I want much to buy, I imagine it may be bought for about £60 sterling. The person who owns it, lives at St Augustine\* in East Florida, I have even wrote to a gentleman who came passenger in the ship with me, to know what it may be bought for. If money can be got out of the rubbish of my affairs to purchase this and three or four negroes I am made for the rest of my days. Upon it I can plant corn, raise tobacco, make indigo; cattle and hoggs I can rear as many as I please, these when killed and salted give a good price at Savannah for the West India market, and the navigation of the river makes the carriage cheap.

My neighbour[6] thinks me a strange man, to live as I do by myself, I have none nigher than two miles except one, and him I must cross the Creek to, which may [be] about 4 times as broad as Pouderhall water, this I seldom do unless it be for to carry over some shirts for his daughters to wash, for which I pay them. I have some times half dozen of these people in my cabbin at a time, they come in when they are hunting their cattle, they will sit 3 or 4 hours, some on a form I have for a seat, others in the bed, listening with open ears, their visits of late have been more frequent, driven by their curiosity. I am always well armed having two guns and two brace of pistols within my reach in the night time. These people are very ignorant of the world and know little more than raising their crops and carrying it to the store, for which they receive goods in return, few of them going to Charlestown and Savannah where they would receive payment in cash or in goods at £50 p[e]r c[en]t less than they pay here, they all complain of the extravagant rates they are obliged to give for goods and indeed I believe this deadens their industry.

There was a strange accident happened the other night. I have not given over my custom of reading in bed yet before I go to sleep. In place of candles I make use of light wood split in long pieces, this is of the heart of the pine. I heard the hen that has the chickens dabbing with her beak and making a great noise, I got out of bed and by help of the light wood found it was a snake endeavouring to get at the chickens, which she defended. He retired at my coming up, I put a piece of wood into the hole where he got in, and went to bed where I fell fast asleep. Some time after I was waked by a noise from that corner and concluded it must be the snake again, I went to the chimney to find if there was any remains of fire where after much blowing I made a shift to make a light. The noise by this time was ceased. I went towards the hen who I found to all appearances dead, the snake was twisted round her

6. Unidentified.

body below the wings and round her neck; with a stick I struck part of him that was disengaged from the hen, whom he directly quit[t]ed, I got another strock which smashed his head, I then threw him out of doors. In the morning I measured him, he was five feet eight inches long. Some of my neighbours who happened to call in told me he was what they call a chicken snake, that his bite was not poisonous but troublesome, however I should not like to have been bite by him, as I would not have known whither it was so or not. You must know my humble cot has but a clay floor and this creature had found its way in at the joints of the loggs.

I forgot to tell you I have an excellent spring of clear water which is all my drink, unless when I go to Augusta where I am treated with wine and punch, this is but seldom for in four months now I have been only three times there although often pressed to come.

What I write is only for Betty,[7] my mother, Nanny and your perusal, if the people with you knew of my strange manner of life they would conclude me mad, therefore for your own sakes keep it to yourselves, for madness in one of a family hurts the rest, you have children with part of the Mylne's blood in them. I can only add the country is most beautifull at present and by not exposing myself in the heat of the day I find I can stand the hot weather very well. I wrote Livingston a little while ago, I sent him a power of attorney from London, their was an absolute necessity to continue him. No other could understand my affairs.

May God Almighty bless our dear Mother, Betty, Nanny and yourself. May your children be a credit and honour to you is the sincere prayer of
Your real friend
        Will$^m$ Mylne

Direct your letter for me at Mr John Hatefields Kings Street Charlestown, as I intend to go there much about the time an answer to this can come.

Do not be dilatory in writing as I can only afford to stay a day or two in Charlestown and if I have not an answer it will be a great disapointment. I find the story of the snake will suffer by the seal-

---

7. Elizabeth Selby,* his sister.

ing. I go to Augusta with this tomorrow when I shall see men I greatly respect for their kindness to me a stranger. Upon second thoughts rather than seal this I put you to a shillings more expence and me half a sheet of paper.

---

Figures given by the governor of Georgia, James Wright, show that between 1753 and 1762 the white population of the colony had almost tripled and the number of blacks had more than quadrupled. The treaty made with the Indians at Augusta in 1763 provided a considerable new area of settlement to absorb some of these people, and it was land of the piedmont region bearing broad-leaved forest, much more fertile than the land taken earlier for plantation in the coastal plain. But still the majority of the area that today forms the state of Georgia was reserved for the Indians, with the Creeks and a small group of Chickasaw claiming the middle and west and the Cherokee the north (as well as most of the area just west of the boundary of the neighboring colony of South Carolina).

The governor wished to have in the backcountry a body of content and well-disciplined white settlers, who would treat the tribes with respect. Both he and the British government considered this necessary for profitable trading and avoidance of war. Such settlers would also themselves contribute to the economic growth of the colony. Wright knew that the London government and the superintendent of Indian affairs, John Stuart, were opposed to any change in the boundaries of settlement negotiated in 1763; yet he needed their cooperation to have the boundaries extended by royal purchase, as required by the proclamation of 1763.

As already noted, many of the white men who arrived in the backcountry after 1763, both settlers and traders, were lacking in discipline—even, it has been said, in the rudiments of civilization—and their relations with the Indians, who were far from deserving the common epithet of "savages," were never really peaceful. Breaches of Stuart's regulations for white traders were partly responsible for this, with some Indians feeling cheated, but the increase in number of traders was also making demands too great on the supply of skins. This resulted in more and more credit being allowed to the Indians for the goods they wanted from the

Augusta traders and merchants, and both Cherokee and Creeks became increasingly indebted to them.

In 1770 the merchants and traders began negotiations with chiefs of the Cherokee about discharging their debts, which were estimated at £45,000. Although the proposal was in line with Governor Wright's hopes for a westward extension of white settlement, the deed that was signed amicably between the chiefs and the traders in February 1771 was a private purchase of Indian land and therefore in breach of the proclamation of 1763. All the Cherokee's debts were to be canceled as payment for an area of sixty miles square, north of the Little River and west of the Savannah. John Stuart's deputy in the Cherokee country, Alexander Cameron,* objected first, and Stuart then declared the deal illegal and referred the problems created—for instance, that the traders had already destroyed their accounts as a seal on the agreement—to London.

Another immediate complication was that the Creeks claimed part of the land involved as theirs by a conquest earlier in the century. This brought those who traded with the Creeks, and the Creeks' large debts, into the discussion, while Governor Wright on leave in England worked hard to obtain the approval of British ministers. He won their approval on condition that the purchase was made by Stuart for the Crown and limited to the area already agreed upon by the Cherokee and traders—Wright having argued for buying more than twice as much. And he was knighted by the king before returning to the colony early in 1773. At a conference at Augusta at the beginning of June the boundaries of the "New Purchase," subsequently called the "Ceded Lands," were agreed upon, but not without ominous signs of resentment on the part of young Creek warriors.

In some negotiations concerned with "settling the accounts" between the Indians and their creditors two men, one of whom was Andrew Robertson,* acted for the governor. For this service Robertson, who was also called Robinson, was related to the Mylnes, and had come into Georgia in 1773 after many years in South Carolina, was later paid by free grants of land.

The Ceded Lands north and west of Augusta amounted to a little over 1.6 million acres. A proclamation by the governor on June 11 declared the land ready for settlement but only to newcomers from outside the province. This condition had been imposed by the London government but was also favored by Wright because he hoped to attract settlers from Great Britain; he wanted no more of the rough and lawless frontiersmen from the colonies to the north. In this respect, the most promising application for land that he received was from a partnership of Jonas Brown of Whitby in Yorkshire, his son Thomas,* and James Gordon* of Orkney.* The opportunities for settlers had probably been made known to Thomas when he petitioned the London government unsuccessfully for a colonial appointment in April 1773.

According to the proclamation of June 11, land grants would consist of one hundred acres for the head of a family, fifty acres each for his wife and for each child, slave, and male indentured servant, and twenty-five acres for each female indentured servant, all indentures to be for a minimum of two years. The purchase prices were set at from one to five shillings per acre, according to the quality of the land, and surveyors and commissioners of sales were appointed. The commissioners met frequently from September 1773 to June 1775 to receive applications and take up deposits, which were generally £2 per hundred acres.

About three hundred applications were approved, most of them for grants of one hundred to three hundred acres and almost all the applicants coming from other colonies, especially North and South Carolina. Two of the largest bids were from James Gordon, granted five thousand acres, and Andrew Robinson, granted two thousand acres, both on November 16, 1773. Gordon, named as from Scotland, undertook to bring into Georgia a "sufficient number of inhabitants" (probably about one hundred) to meet the conditions of the grant and Robinson, from South Carolina, was to settle his present family including five children and ten slaves immediately and bring further slaves to the number required by his grant. For both applicants the lands were reserved until the required numbers of settlers arrived, the reservation to hold for periods up to one year. Gordon was to pay a deposit; although only he is mentioned in the records of the commissioners for Ceded Lands, his grants were for the partnership of Brown and Gordon. The wording of the record can also be interpreted as indicating that he was not yet in the colony. The record states that a deposit was also due from Robinson, but later evidence shows that he received the land free in lieu of payment for his former service to the governor.

Indentured servants were immigrants who could not afford the cost of removal to America and who, to pay for their passages, bound themselves and in many cases their whole families to service for a period of from two to seven years, during which they were entitled to no wages but provided with food, accommodation, and basic clothing. Moreover, their indentures to serve could be bought and sold, and so the conditions under which they worked, as well as those under which they were carried to the colonies, might be no better than those of slaves. Brown and Gordon's servants were bound for only three years and were allowed fifteen acres per man, ten for a wife, and five for each child over ten years of age, for their own use and profit. This land was to be rent free for five years, one shilling per acre per annum for a second five years, and thereafter two shillings. A few of these servants were recruited from Yorkshire and embarked at Whitby, but the greater proportion came from the North of Scotland and embarked at Gordon's island home, Orkney. The first party, with forty-eight men and women and twenty-six children, left Whitby on Jonas Brown's ship, the *Marlborough*, on August 12, 1774, and reached Savannah on November 17. Gordon had preceded them to Georgia and was already in residence at New Richmond,* a fine house and plantation on the South Carolina side of the Savannah River about five miles upstream from Augusta. Thomas Brown arrived from England with the party of servants.

The governor had attempted to provide for the safety of new settlers. One of his commissioners for land grants, Edward Barnard,* was also commissioned on September 6, 1773, as captain of a troop of "horse rangers" to garrison and police the Ceded Lands. They were enlisted under full military discipline and numbered seventy to eighty men, including the captain, other officers, sergeants, and a surgeon. They were to occupy several posts, the chief of which was Fort James,* at the confluence of the Broad River with the Savannah. The order for this fort to be constructed described it as "one hundred twenty feet square, with four bastions made of square logs, two of them to be covered and two left open at the top; the curtains between the bastions to be lined by punchions; officers houses, barracks, and goalhouse [sic] and magazine"; but whether it was built exactly like that is doubtful. A colorful uniform for the rangers was also ordered: "A blue coat faced with red and a red jacket and blue cloth boots or spatterdashes made to fit the leg edged with red and gartered with a black strap and buckle . . . and breeches either blue cloth or buckskin."

Settlement in the Ceded Lands began but was very soon interrupted. On December 25, 1773, a war party of Creek Indians attacked and massacred the family of William White, an immigrant from North Carolina, on his holding near the headwaters of the Ogeechee River. On January 14, 1774, another party of Creeks attacked a group of settlers working on the construction of a stockade fort at a site in the southwest of the Ceded Lands, west of Wrightsborough.* Seven of the twenty settlers were killed and five others wounded. Again, on January 23, a force of Georgia militia and rangers was ambushed and routed by a Creek war party; most of the militiamen deserted, and settlers in the Ceded Lands fled to the safety of stockade forts on the south side of Little River and also to Augusta itself, where at least four houses were fortified with stockades. Settlement in the Ceded Lands virtually ceased, and even the squatters left the area.

In March two Creek chiefs were killed by white men in separate incidents. Big Elk was ambushed by a party of frontiersmen while engaged in an attempt to persuade Cherokees to join in the Creek attacks; Mad Turkey, in contrast, had gone to Augusta to talk of peace when he was murdered by an angry blacksmith. On April 14 Emistisiguo,* a respected Creek headman, with other chiefs met the governor in Savannah and agreed to call on the Creek Nation to cease hostilities, promising to report their response to the governor within three moons. It was actually more than six months before any new assurance of safety could be given to prospective settlers.

---

To M$^r$ W$^m$ Mills,[8]
    Charlestown, South Carolina

                                          Powderhall
                                        May 17    1774

My Dearest Willy

    with the utmost anxiety and the greatest aprehension for your welfare, do I sit down to write you—good god, what can be the meaning of your silence—of all the letters I have wrote you (and I have wrote regularly the first of every month since your departure) I have received none, but one dated from Charlestown Sep$^{tmb}$ the 21—in it you refer me to a letter sent by a Scotch ship for your determination, this letter I have never received, nor care about[9]—so I had received some since that time, leting me at least know that you was well and in the land of the living.

    All remains here just as you left us—my Lord Elliok's decisions is still delayed, owing to a quarell between the fewers[10] and the town, this to me is mortifying *to even write you* after so long space of expectation, yet I would hope this August vacation will put an end to it—he allows to every person the validity of your claim but for one reason or another declars it would be improper for him to decide.

    The Bashaw[11] has sent word that he is to be here in August, I shall take myself owt of the way as usuall. I have got a good deal of the wood sold[12] and shall [ac]count with you for it.

8. Anne's decision to use the surname "Mills," thought by William to have resulted in the loss of many letters (see page 40), is unexplained.
9. September 21 cannot be the date of a letter from William at Charleston. If December 21, 1773, is substituted, the "letter sent by a Scotch ship" should be William's letter of August 29 and September 4, 1773, presumably committed at the port of London to a ship bound for Leith. It contained his "determination" about handling of his financial affairs (see letter of September 4, 1773). His later denial (see letter of October 13, 1774) of having sent a letter by a Scottish ship appears to be a failure of memory.
10. "Feuars" were the citizens who had taken house plots in the New Town extension of Edinburgh by feu contract, the Scottish system of land tenure. As the town council wished the extension to succeed and the bridge was the new feuars' access from the old town, they were sensitive to the feuars' complaints when arranging for repairs to the bridge.
11. Anne's frequent name for Robert—a Turkish title for a civil or military governor (modern "pasha"), with connotations of haughty behavior.
12. Wood used for scaffolding, etc., could be sold after the completion of a bridge contract. Presumably William had left a quantity to be sold by Anne.

Little Will is my constant companion, he is a fine boy, lively to excess yet loves me and dreads my frown—my mother is very fond of him, yet complains that I spoil him with indulgence—poor little fellow, I think often of you when I look at him, I have him at a reading school in town and have begune to teach him writing myself when finished with his reading; shall put him to a proper school for it—I dress him plain and neat.

I have conjured you in all my other letters to draw upon me for money, again I repeat it. Depend on my love and care for everything in my power for your interest, heaven knows the anxiety your silence has cost me. I still hope that change of place and accident is the cause of it. I shall direct this to M$^r$ Hatfield to whose care you ordered your letters.

Farewell my dearest Willy—and relieve my anxitiety [sic] and believe in every change of situation most sincerely and

Affectionately your<br>Anne Mylne

[on verso] Your mother is in good health, but very unhappy on your account—the Selbys are all well—Capt. Clarke is dead of a short ffever about a month ago—the Browns* are just as formerly. Again I intreat write by every opportunity—you cannot think how unhappy you make me.

---

To   Miss Ann Mylne
      at Mr Robert Selby's,* Baillie Fyfe's Closs,
                   Edinburgh, North Britain
  p[e]r the *Daniel,* Capt. Gearviss,
  via Liverpool.

               New Richmond on Savannah, 3 miles from Augusta
               1$^{st.}$ Sept$^r$ 1774

My Dearest Nanny

What a deal of uneaseness to us both might have been prevented by understanding one another. I don't remember that you was to address me by the name of Mills, theirs our ill luck, and all your letters must now be lying in the Post Office at Charlestown, or perhaps satisfying the curiosity of some idle person. You must write no more to me untill I let you know, for long before I can receive an answer to this I shall leave this place, for several reasons as you will learn afterwards. This is the worst place I believe in the world for either sending of or receiving letters, their is no Post, and one must wait the going down of some one to Charlestown; I got away a large packet to you in the month of May last, which will ere now fully satisfy you of what I had gone throw to its date. Another packet lay no less than three months at Augusta, this last went away as I understand about the middle of July last, I wish I had it again. 1$^{st.}$ I cannot receive your answer here, 2$^{dly}$ I wrote for many things I shall have no use for now I intend to come away, which I hope this may come time enough to prevent you cause making or sending. All I shall want is half a dozen of good shirts, and half dozen of course [coarse?], tow pair of shoes, a pair of stocking breeches black, these send to Will$^m$ Mylne, to the care of M$^r$ John Hatfield, Kings Street Charlestown, no more fictitious names, I am known in every great town.

   I wrote to Selby and Livingston, which last I wish I had back. To you and Bob I laid down a scheme of life which now I must relinquish. In my former I amused you how agreably I lived by myself with my gun, fishing, and garden; I had spent near five months in this agreable manner of life when, as the Devil would have it, 1$^{st.}$ the gentlemen of Augusta took it into their heads they would come up and see me, this gave me great uneaseness but I always got it parried, 2$^{dly}$ our cousin Robinson came up from Savannah, on his way to view his lands on Broad River, M$^r$ Gordon who has large tracts taken up there was to be in company, they sent a message they were coming to see me, this would not suit as no body knew how I lived but some of my country neighbours. I went immediatly to Augusta and had the good fortune to meet them on the road coming up, they returned to M$^r$ M$^c$Kays, when they insisted on me taking the journey with them, they would take no refusal and got me perswaded against my reason—it was the middle of July, and the heats at the greatest hight. I trusted to the goodness of my constitution, from the manner of life I had followed I was in excellent health; Robinson promised we should not travell after nine in the morning, and to set out two hours before sun set. Robinson is one of those beings that when they cannot widdle into the management of great things takes up with small, he accordingly was manager, their scheme was to get me to pitch upon proper situations for their houses, offices, and servants houses, and afterwards to draw plans of them.

We set out well mounted and armed, a servant with us, a pack horse loaded with provisions, and a tent to camp under at night. I shall not trouble you with our route. On the second day I fell sick. We came to Fort James at the mouth of Broad River, where a party of the rangers was ordered for an escort. The 4$^{th}$ day after leaving the Fort I was attacked by a fever, I still continued to travell examining the nature and soil of the lands which are pleasantly situate on Broad River, which runs above sixty miles before it falls into Savannah. We came to a cabbin where a family lived, at this place I determined to stop. I had before this examined M$^r$ Gordon's grounds, his lay nighest, and was able to form some judgement of them so as to make plans and mark situations. I told Robinson I could proceed no further, this freted him much as he was anxious to have his matters properly laid out, I stopt his mouth by telling him it was his bad management in travelling in the middle of the day that had brought this sickness upon me. He was obliged to set out without me, the distance was but 15 miles but I was very bad. Here we staid two days, Robinson endeavouring to get a promise from me to come up again with him in the month of Nov$^r$ at which time he proposes to bring up his wife and family, to a good house he has taken about 40 miles above Augusta on the River Savannah, but this I shall not do. We got back to Fort James where I got some doctor stuff that did me no good, we now crossed over to Carolina (I should have told you that is [*sic*] from these lands we rode over the people had all run away and few returned since the Indians committed the murders) and came to the French setlement, where they are proposing to make wine under the direction of a Mon$^{sr}$ S$^t$ Piere.* There are many of that nation there, who have a parson and doctor. The hard frost killed all their grapes and I question if they succeed, the Spring comes early and things comes forward, a frost often succeeds that nips the fruit in the bud, which was the case this year, this happens to many usefull things in this country.

About this time an express came to Robinson, informing [him] that George Baillie* & Willy Baillie* were come to Augusta and wanted him down on business. They sent compts. and wanted much to see me. Willy had come out and entered attorney, his

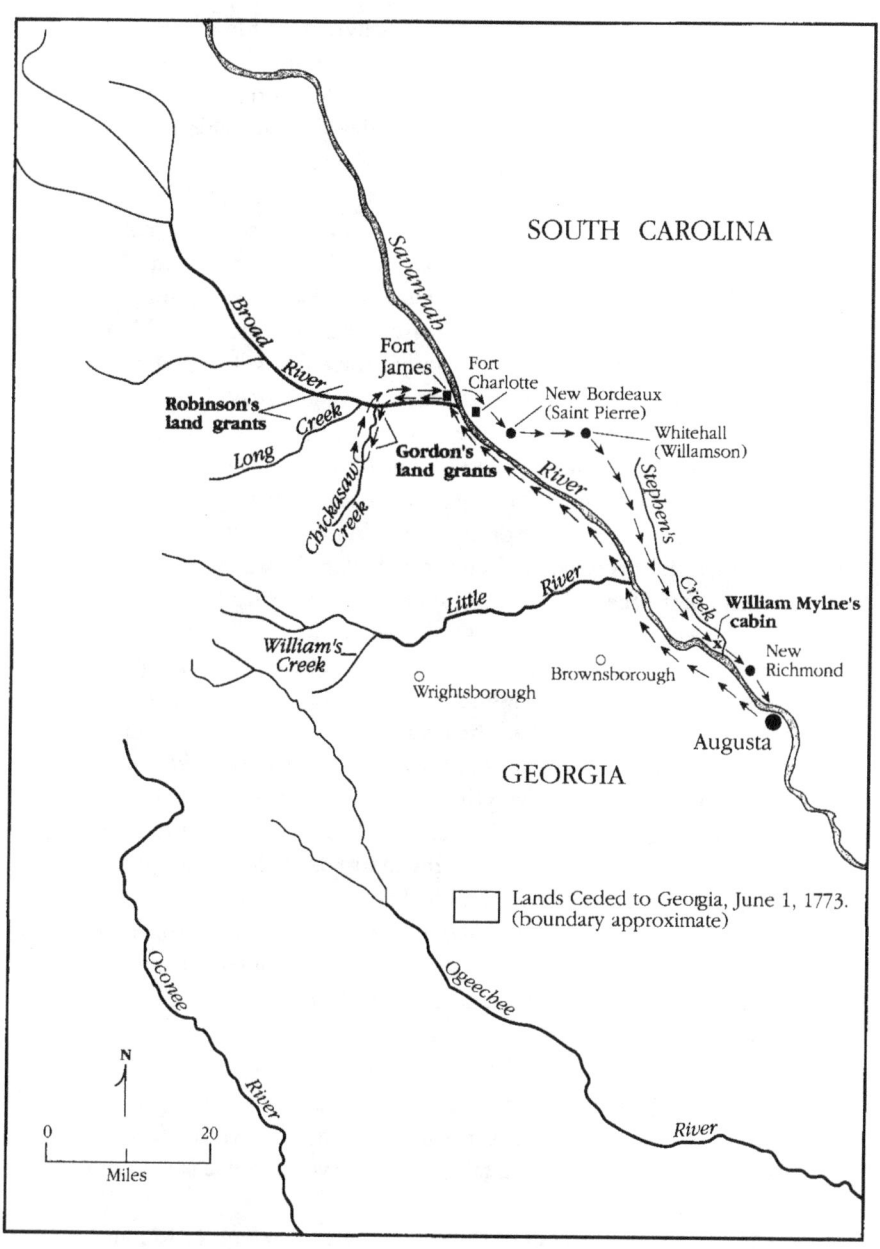

Map of William Mylne's journey to the Ceded Lands

uncles wife and him quarelled, I had received a long letter from him telling of his intention of going home & following his old scheme of portrait painting; in answer, I endeavoured to do diswade [sic] him, he begged letters for that purpose which I refused. I believe he had come up on purpose to see me.

We came next to the plantation of a M$^r$ Williamson,* here I fell extremly ill, they two gentlemen waited a day for me, when I insisted upon their going on without me. At this gentleman's I was taken care of with the utmost humanity, having everything the plantation could afford and a negro servant to attend me. Here I continued seven days, when I thought myself so well I might venture to set out although entreated to stay some days longer—they insisted I should take a servant along with me, which I would upon no account allow. I set out for one M$^r$ Purvis, and rode 25 miles without eating, and I may say drinking, for the great heats had dryed up most of the springs. I was frightned that I would loose myself for it is very difficult to travell in the woods, their are so many paths that intersect one another that missing the one one should keep, one may go God knows where. Well, much fatigued I got to Purves who was not at home. I had a letter for him, I got his overseer, everything was locked up. I staid here all night and would have staid longer had the landlord been at home. I set out and after riding 18 miles got to my castle, I turned my horse loose, opened my door, found everything solitary, I struck up a fire, hung on my pot, catched a chicken, plucked him etc., put him in with a bit of bacon, spread down my matress, lay down, happy in the weak situation I was in that I had got home.

I staid four days in my old manner, very weak. During this I received no less than four letters from M$^r$ Gordon insisting upon coming down, and once he came up himself but I took care he could not cross the creek having my canoe full of rain water. Luckly the Baillies and Robinson were gon to Savannah. I came to this place 3 weeks ago, it is a perfect paradise, the house is the best in these parts, situate on the banks of the river 3 miles from Augusta. I have had again a relapse of the fever which is now stopt by the bark [13] and am picking up again fast.

My reasons for leaving this place are these, although I had half

---

13. "Jesuit's bark," also called "Peruvian bark" and obtained from cinchona trees, contained quinine. Its use may have been learned from the Indians.

dozen of negreos [*sic*] I could not pretend to keep company and entertain them in return, M$^r$ Gordon would be nigh me, Robinson has bought a plantation in this parts, the gentlemen of Augusta would all be nigh and although I was at the distance of forty miles it would be the same, they think nothing of a visit at that distance staying a fortnight on a visit at a time. I have had offers of reccomendation to settle in Charlestown but I could not live there six months. I shall leave this in Dec$^r$ for Charlestown, from whence I shall go to some of the large towns to the northward where it is very healthy and living cheap, and attempt my proffesion, in which I have reason to think I shall succeed. My health will soon be reastblished by the cold weather coming in.

I received yours inclosed in one from M$^r$ Hatfeild four days ago, its date is May the 17$^{th}$—you wonder I have not mentioned it sooner, but you have guessed I had got it—I am extremly sorrow for the distress you have been thrown into for my wellfare it has arose from the particular situations I have been obliged to go throw and the tedious conveyance of letters.

Lord Elliock's decision I dont expect so soon as you do, the Town will find means to fight it of[f]. I am much obliged to you for the care you take of my affairs, but take care of his honour who will look sharply into things. I received a civil letter from him a few days ago with offers of services, with a new factory for Livingston, as some have disputed to pay. I shall answer his letter in the same civil manner, he says he would have reccomended Italy and could have got an employment for me in which he had no concern—but I have had enough of his employments. I desired you to send me out a bill for fifty pounds, it is more money than I shall want now I have changed my scheme of life. I suppose you have done this at the time you received the letter, if not it will be embarassing, not for the money, for I am in no want, but in detaining me here. It might occurr to you that I could get no money on a bill drawn upon you as you are not known.

How happy am I My Dear Mother keeps her health so well. God bless her. Take care of poor Willy, we may make something of him. Adieu,

    God bless you,
        Will$^m$ Mylne

My hand shakes much

A sense of scandal swept through all the colonies when Boston Port was closed on June 1, 1774, by an act of the British Parliament. In Georgia, as elsewhere, there were strong political reactions during the summer and fall. For the Georgians, however, there was a real threat of war with the Creek Nation, and many believed that the safety of the backlands could only be assured by the arrival of a British military force. Expressions of loyalty to Britain were therefore heard as often, and in the backlands initially more often, than sentiments of liberty. The governor begged the British commander-in-chief in the colonies repeatedly for regular soldiers to be sent but without success. Georgia sent no representatives to the First Continental Congress, convened at Philadelphia on September 5.

On August 10 a meeting called by Whigs at Tondee's Tavern in Savannah passed resolutions of protest against Britain's encroachments on the liberties of the colonies. Immediately afterward, a body of Loyalists in Savannah signed and published a declaration of dissent from these resolutions, one of the signatories being Andrew Robertson. Similar dissent was heard and Loyalist resolutions passed at meetings representing the town and district of Augusta, Saint Paul's Parish, Kyoka and Broad River settlements, Saint George's Parish, Queensborough,* and Wrightsborough, and all were reported in the *Georgia Gazette* between August 17 and October 12. The Saint Paul's Parish resolution was signed, among others, by Robert Mackay, Edward Barnard, Andrew McLean, John Francis Williams,* James Gordon, and Daniel Waiscoat.* They protested that their representatives had been excluded from the Whigs' meeting at Savannah on August 10, where they would have voted against the resolutions; they cited the great danger to them of an Indian war "unless we receive such powerful aid and assistance as none but Great Britain can give"; and they declared their "dissent to all resolutions by which His Majesty's favour and protection might be forfeited."

Some of the signatories to the Loyalist resolutions—but none of those listed above—were men who within a year became supporters of the revolutionary movement and even leaders of its forces. This was a natural outcome of vacillation by Wright and Stuart between support for the traders' interests and encouragement of settlers in the backcountry. To put extra pressure on the Creeks after Emistisiguo's promise in April to seek a return to peaceful coexistence, Wright persuaded his fellow southern governors in the early summer to suspend all trade with the Creek Nation. This was a severe blow to all traders, and although some defied the ban, the Creeks were more or less starved of ammunition and other goods at a time when they were subject to attacks by the Choctaw from the west. Tension was suddenly eased one day in August when nine Creeks arrived unannounced at Robert Mackay's house in Augusta just as he was sitting down to dinner with Edward Barnard, captain of the rangers in the Ceded Lands, and David Taitt,* Stuart's deputy to the Creek Nation. They had come to tell Taitt that they wanted peace and the resumption of trade.

When Wright and Stuart met the chiefs in Savannah on October 20, however, as well as lifting the trade ban they confirmed the boundaries set by the Treaty of Augusta in June 1773 and undertook specifically that white men would not hunt between the Ogeechee and the Oconee rivers. In this they were acting on the expressed wish of the Augusta traders that the Creeks should retain their hunting grounds and rejecting pressure from settlers and the Georgia Assembly to insist on a new cession of Creek land between the rivers—a cession that Wright himself had hoped for but was denied in 1773. In succeeding months Wright never regained the goodwill of the existing settlers. Neither the influx of British settlers with Thomas Brown, James Gordon, and others late in the year and in 1775 nor the friendship with Indians that he had won and tried later to exploit could sustain Wright's rule in the backlands when most of the settlers took the side of the rebels.

---

New Richmond 13$^{th}$ Oct$^r$ 1774

My Dearest Nany,

It was with the greatest pleasure I read yours of the 28$^{th}$ of July. You acted wisely in the letter of credit in place of a bill, I would fain hope I shall have little occassion for it, I have learned that 12 & 15 pr ct may sometimes be had for a draft on London. I wrote you about five weeks ago in answer to your former, in it I gave you my reasons for leaving this place. The money requisite to settle a plantation so as to be comfortable is considerable and one must live on an equality with one's friends, this would be expensive; if I was to settle as a planter in this country it would be near Agusta, where the principal people lives handsomly, these would visit me in their turn. I have considered things attentively, and upon the whole I find my prudentest step is to follow my proffesion in some of the great towns to the northward, where money is a thousand times plentier than here and where I stand little chance of competitors. If I fail in the attempt, it will be attended with no more expence than my living, which will not be great as it is a most plentifull country. Philadelphia, or New York, are the places I intend to try. The expence of travelling will not be much and no man can travel cheaper than I can, and save appearances at the same time. I think I have as much money left of what I brought out as will carry me to the northward and support me some time there, so possibly I may have no occassion for the letter of credit, which will be the case if I fall into employment soon, but I must find some one in Charlestown, when I go down, that will give me a credit on New York, so that I may be enabled to draw from there in case I want. Whether this can be effectuated without drawing from Charlestown I cannot say, which, if I do, will be for very little.

It is a much more healthy country I am going to than this, the great people of this province going there to pass the summer once in two or three years for the preservation of their health. I have had a very severe fit of sickness, the fever and ague, it lasted first and last above three months, I was twice reduced to skin and bone and so weak that I could scarce walk across the room. I have been most tenderly taken care of by M$^r$ Gordon, who is proprietor of this place. I must have doctors, hang them all, it was against my inclination to have any but my friends insisted, they stuffed me with Jesuits bark till my stomach revolted and threw it back. There were numbers of people sick of the same disorder. I dont think much of me having it as strangers, first or last, are subject to it and it is what they call a seasoning to the country. Doctor's fees, money in presents to attendants and travelling my last journey, took away more cash than I wished for, however I have still thirty pounds left counting my horse at ten pounds. Thank God the cool weather is set in, the fever and ague gone, and I can mount my horse. In two months I shall leave this, so that I may get to the northward by the end of the winter.

I wish much I had not wrote for the things, but if they do come out they will be safe enough as I can get them from Charlestown. The expence of them will be saved you, as I expect my last would come time enough to prevent your causing them to be made.

Willy Baillie who left this some time ago will be by this in London. If he follows his plan of painting he will get himself introduced to M$^r$ Strange's* family, to whom he will tell where I am, this will contradict what I find his honour was very officious in, by letting the publick know I was gone to Italy.

Now for your letter. Why do you weep at my hardships? I assure you I had much diversion when in good health. Why are you so anxious about my preservation? Health I value, but life I don't, I am naturally to[o] impatient to bear a lingering disorder. I was offered strong reccomendations to settle in Charlestown and was assured in a few years I should make a fortune, but the very thoughts of being attacked by lingering sickness dettered me. I wrote to Charlestown to enquire about your letters and I hope to get them. I never did write by a Scotch ship [14] and it was as you surmised. My situation at my Hermitage was the most pleasant that I could be in, considering the temper of mind I was possessed of at that time, hating all mankind; I thank God the humanity and politness of the gentlmen of Agusta have recalled me to society. You are much mistaken in my being handless, for I can cook victuals as well as any American backwoodsman, where often in the woods we have taken up our quarters near a spring of fresh water, made a fire and dressed what we had to eat, I found it necessary in my situation to learn those things and soon became a profficient.

The only thing I wish my affairs settled for is to get free of his honour, I hope as you say it will be soon. I could ask many questions, but it would [be] too long a time before I could receive an answer, besides you must write no more till you hear from me. I cannot understand what you mean of my granting a factory to his honour, nobody has a power of acting but Livingston, I think my letters from London should have informed of that, and my reasons for granting that power to him. If their is not money arises sufficient to pay the debts, he can only come in for his proportion,

14. See page 39.

I hope this will not be the case and everyone will be paid, if it should be prove[n] otherwise, I hope God Almighty will prosper my endeavours to do it.

I have given out to my friends I intend to go home and come out next or the year following. M^rs Mackay* told me yesterday that if I brought you out they would endeavour to make the place as agreable to you as possible. She came from the northward with her daughter M^rs Williams* whom a rascal of this country who went there for his health married, he used her extremly ill which has ruined her health and she was forced to leave him. She lives with her mother whom M^r Mackay married, she is older than him, they are extremly well bred and very civil and polite to strangers, their house is the great resort of the best people, I am always welcome to a bed when I go down. Mungo lives with them, he was not able to follow me in my travelling any longer. M^rs Williams is very fond of him, young Baillie it seems knew him again and that, no doubt, would bring on some questions from the ladies about you.

I assure [you] if ever I am possesed of a sum of money I intend to have a plantation in these parts, but good land and properly situate is growing dearer every day. If that is the case, on a certain event which I hope is far off,[15] you shall come over and reign over the negroes, you have no sisters in laws to be afraid of. I have now, by my residence and almost constant stirring about when well, seen all the different methods of cultivation of the produce of the country. You will see by my scheme their will be no occassion for servants to come out; what you write about the Orkney people surprises me a good deal, if they were bound to America how came they to Leith? for all outward bound from that part to these parts make the Orkneys. M^r Gordon at whose house I live, and of which I am master at present, is gone to Savannah in the expectation of the arrival of a ship full of Orkney servants, if this should prove the ship he expects it will be a great loss and disapointment to him. It is a bad scheme in bringing out white servants, in a short time they see how easily the labouring people (who does but half work) live, they have from 1 sh 6^d to 2 sh a day [16] and their

---

15. The death of his mother.
16. Wages of one shilling and sixpence to two shillings per day.

victuals found, this is paid in cattle, hogs and corn (the planters having little money, or merchants either, for most is managed by truck); with these they pass the winter. A man that works three months can live the rest of the year idle; the newcomers see this and run of[f], when they are not easily found again. Negroes are the properest for a planter, with a white man as overseer.

Your letter came very quick which is oweing to a post being opened betwixt Charlestown and Savannah. Some of my letters have been three months in one place for want of an opportunity as you may see by the dates.

Copy letter from Brother.    London, March 7th 1744 [*sic*, 1774] D<sup>r</sup> Brother, I received all your letters—some of old date (*I do not know what he means by this for I only wrote one at London when I came away, of which I sent a copy to you, and a few lines from Charlestown to let him know where I was in case there was any papers to send out for me to sign*). As I feel myself entirely satisfied with my own conduct I shall not now take up any part of their contents, and which from your present situation would now serve no purpose to discuss. When you return to your country and friends it will then be more proper. At present I shall hold the silence you have imposed on me.

I received your letter of Sept<sup>r</sup> last and find thereby you suppose I should have been against your going abroad; in which you was mistaken. I should have reccomended *Italy indeed* as a much more proper place and fitter for your own purpose. I cannot help thinking that still it would be a more proper place than America. I could have found you employment for that purpose, without your being under any obligation to me. To go abroad, I thought, was *now* become necessary and I think it might have been usefull in a future prospect of life. I thought it necessary to inform the publick of your absence, for your own sake; and therefore inserted in the newspapers you was gone to Italy to resume your studys—and there they suppose you now to be.

I should not have troubled you with the inclosed, but that M<sup>r</sup> Livingston (who desires to be remembered to you and to whom I sent your letter of attorney) finds it necessary to have more full powers with respect to the receipt of debts; as one was questioned by the agents of the D[uke] of Argyle,* notwithstanding they paid the money. As to a *better security* for myself, I shall consider M$^r$ Livingston's integrity as the best. When a final settlement of your affairs are had, you will then know what my intentions always have been, since the bridge affairs became a losing matter, or seemed to be so. He has already proceeded a great way in settling all other affairs, paying some and receiving the money of others. £100 will finish the whole, I observe, and he shall have it. I mean the whole of the simple debts. As to the moneys due to Selby and your sister, as I have known nothing of them till now, so I intend not to meddle with them. I have directed M$^r$ Livingston to receive the rents and pay the taxes and keep a separate account of the produce u[n]mixed with any other affair. And out of that produce to pay Selby and your sister the interest regularly, for their respective sums. In doing this, he finds himself at a loss, by 2 memorandums in your book of accounts of work done for Mess$^{rs}$ Bell and Kerr. Do you mean he should send them discharged accounts? and M$^r$ Read, who can't pay any rent at all, says he had always his house rent free from you. When he can he will pay, he says from Whitsunday 1773.

Bridge affairs stand as they did. The arbiter is not well, and had like to have died. The[y] have fitted up and finished one end of the bridge with butresses and proposes to do the other this ensuing season. Ferguson* has gained his law suit against the town about building his few [17] in Cleland's Yards, before the House of Lords here. If you want any of my services in the place where you are, you will command me as I am ever yours, Signed R. Mylne PS Everybody remains the same as before.

In answer to his letter I wrote a few lines, being very bad at the time, and sent the paper for Livingston, signed and witnessed. I declined any favour or services he could make me, and wished that my affairs were soon ended, that he might have his money. I begged he would not interest himself about me at all and to look upon me as a man that was dead to him and to my country.

May God Almighty preserve my Dear Mother, tell her I hope to see her yet in a different situatiation [*sic*] than that in which I

---

17. Correctly *feu*, a portion of land held by feu contract from a "superior" who retained limited rights of control on its use.

left her. Remember me in the kindest manner to the Selby family. I wish much that all the letters that are coming out may arrive before I leave this. Tell Miss Bruce Strange,* as she is in the secret, that a Mr. Jas. Gordon, who is from Orkney and is one of her great friends, and I have drank her health a hundred times in these back wood lands, present her my best respects, as also to Mr. Livingston who you say is one friend, few I have indeed. I am glad to hear poor Willy is well and does well. I hope he will be something in society, this is the country for such as him that labours under the stigma of a bastard.

We are to have peace here. A number of Indians have gone to settle matters with the Governor at Savannah. Had they known their own strength they could have drove everyone out of Georgia, there are no troops here and when demanded were refused, Government is so enraged at the behaviour of the Americans. The militia were frightned and would not have stood on fire. The trade has been stop[p]ed there some months with them.

I have a strong temtation for a man of my turn of mind. The Deputy Superintendent for Indian Affairs (who is at present at Savannah) wants me much to go with him to the Creek nation, from thence he proposes to go to Mobile,* from that to Pensacola* and New Orleans* at the mouth of the Missisppii, belonging to the Spaniards, and so to fort Natchez* a good way up; but I will resist the temptation. Believe me to be
    Your loving brother and sincere friend
             Will$^m$ Mylne

---

The deputy superintendent of Indian affairs mentioned was certainly John Stuart's deputy to the Creeks, David Taitt. The journey would follow immediately the nation's treaty with John Stuart and Sir James Wright on October 20 and may have been planned for follow-up negotiations or as a timely goodwill visit.

When Thomas Brown's party of seventy-four settlers arrived in Georgia a month later, he and James Gordon led them to Augusta but not onward to the lands by the Broad River and Chickasaw Creek, which Gordon had reserved for them a year earlier. It probably still seemed risky to take newcomers into the Ceded Lands, and they were placed instead on a substantial property that Brown had acquired in a well-settled area by the forks of Kiokee

Creek about twenty miles west-northwest of Augusta. This tract probably contained about 2,500 acres, on which Brown planned a settlement to be called Brownsborough. He set the new arrivals to work building a plantation house for him and other farmhouses or cottages—thirty-six in number, according to later documents—and a barn as well as stables for the fine horses he had brought from England.

The governor issued another proclamation on October 24 that those applicants for whom lots had been reserved in the Ceded Lands must take out their grants and occupy the land within six months or their reservations would be canceled and their deposits forfeited. Some must have responded, but few if any seem to have made any further payment. Only a paltry sum had been collected in deposits, and although the accounts of traders (and merchants) who claimed debts due to them from the Indians were examined by officials in Savannah early in 1775, it is doubtful if any received payment.

A rumor began to spread among the settlers that the British, having favored the traders once, were willing to do so again by arming the Indians against the revolutionaries, which stimulated a new fear of the Indians and growing hatred of England. Groups such as the Sons of Liberty began to harass the Loyalists and no real peace came to the backlands before the end of the Revolution in 1782. The fertility and prosperity of the area survived the war, however, and Augusta emerged as the capital of the new state of Georgia.

William Mylne had stuck to his plan and left the Augusta area quietly at the end of 1774.

---

[Stamped "CHARLESTOWN, IA, 4"]

To Miss Ann Mylne
    at M<sup>r</sup> Robert Selby's, Baillie Fyfe's Closs,
        Edinburgh, North Britain.

                        CharlesTown
                      [4 January?, 1775]

My Dearest Nanny,
    I wrote you from New Richmond by a gentleman who had come up that way, and was returning to this town. I was just beg-

gining to recover from the fever and ague which had reduced me very low; some time after I rode as far as the Congarees,* about eighty miles distant, to shake of[f] the dregs of the disorder. It had the desired effect, I have recovered every day since and am now in as good a state of health as I ever remember. When I came back I took myself to my solitary life in my hermit[a]ge, much against the inclination of my friends. There I lived in my old manner till eight days before I left Augusta, which I passed at M$^r$ Mackay's. I was offered letters to some of the best people in this place, these I declined as no way answering my situation, they would have led to too expensive a way of life.

It was with great regret I left my cottage, I assure you the pleasantest time of my life for a long time past was spent there, secluded in a manner from all the world, except a few whose disinterested friendship made them still more dear to a mind cut and slashed by the villany of mankind. I left them in the belief that I was to return the beggining of next winter, in consequence of which there is a commission which I must beg you will execute, this I will mention after.

I left Augusta and rode down the Georgia side of the river for above 80 miles, through an extensive pine barren in which were few plant[at]ions, those being mostly on the side of the river; this I passed at a ferry called the Three Sisters,* and came into Carolina. All the way on this side to Charlestown (which was about 160 miles) there were large plantations for rice and indigo, except about 40 miles of uncultivate country; this is but a short skech, as I am afraid my paper will admit of no other. Mungo and I travelled by ourselves, except the two last days when we had company enough, indeed we are so much accustomed to live, and travel by ourselves that we seem a separate species of the human and canin[e] creation. My horse and the poor creature have contracted a strict alliance and friendship together; whenever he was attacked by the currs from the houses he took shelter among the horses legs and none durst attack him. Although Mungo performed this last journey with great spirit, I am much afraid the long one I am about to undertake will prove to[o] many for him, he is now growing old; when we are parted I shall lose a faithfull friend. My journey is near 800 miles long through one half South and all North Carolina, Virginia, Maryland, Pensilvania, to New York where I propose trying my fortune. Allthough this is commonly down [done?] by sea, yet as I have a horse I intend to ride it, if I sold my horse here I would not get nigh what he is worth, the market being overstocked at present.

Sometime before I left Georgia, the Governor concluded a peace with the Indians, without having the satisfaction he ought to have had, they will keep this no longer than it is for their own interest. The Creeks were hard pushed by the Chactaws with whom they are at war and wanted ammunition, the trade being stoped. The Governor could get no assistance from England on account of the difference that subsists betwixt America and her, the Province was too weak of itself to begin a war which must have ended in their ruin, the back parts remained in an unsetled state, the people being afraid to live on them; these reasons forced both parties into a compromise which the Creeks will keep no longer than they can make peace with the Chactaws, this they are endeavouring to do. The Virginians are at war with the Shawanese* and have had one brush in which a good many were killed on both sides, it was not decisive and here they expect the news of another battle soon. Should the Shawanese get the advantage it is more than probable they will be joined by the Cherokees which will greatly embarass the Southern provinces. All the Americans seem obstinate not to make any concessions to England, in every place wherein I have been they talk of fighting to the last man for their liberties and properties—should a general Indian war and a civil one take place at the same time, this will be a terrible scourge and I shall be in a fine situation, but I hope neither will happen.

As soon as I came here I enquired for letters but there was none. Your former letters must have gone to pot. In case any came to Augusta, I beged M$^r$ Mackay to send them addressed to me at Pouderhall; open them, or any others, for several said they would write me, our cousin Robinson for one, whom I met on the road from Savannah to Augusta, he expressed much friendship for me and would fain [have] perswaded me to go and live at his house in Savannah till his return. M$^r$ Hatfeild at whose house I lodge is very carefull of everything that concerns me, he showed me your letter to him, it is wrote in a stile very proper for the matter you wanted to know of and the kind concern you expressed in it on my account pleased him and affected me very much.

Before I left Augusta I gave M$^r$ Mackay most of the money I had left. As he from what I had given out expected I was going directly home [he] beged I would execute a comission for him, which you will observe by the following memorandum copied from his

| | |
|---|---|
| Amount of an order on M<sup>r</sup> Ogilvey* | £205-18-8 |
| Deduct what M<sup>r</sup> Mylne paid | 120- 0-0 |
| Ballance | £ 85-18-8 |

£ 85.18.8<sup>d</sup> South Carolina currency is equal to Twelve Pounds five shillings and eight pence sterling—M<sup>r</sup> Mackay requests the favour of M<sup>r</sup> Mylne after he gets to Edinburgh to inclose ten pounds sterling of the above in a cover directed to M<sup>r</sup> Francis Mackay* at Browan near Wick in Caithness—the other forty-five shilings he beggs M<sup>r</sup> Mylne to lay out in as much Scotch carpeting as will cover a floor 26 by 20 feet. The paper for said room M<sup>r</sup> Mylne will purchase and bring out with him for which M<sup>r</sup> Mackay will thankfully pay him.

Now what I must beg of you is to send in a cover the ten pounds sterling mentioned above and desire him to let you know if he received it, in the same cover send also the inclosed letter. The carpeting I beg you buy and, although it should cost a little more than forty five shillings, lay it out, as I am under great obligations to M<sup>r</sup> Mackay. This money prevents me making use of the letter of credit you sent out sometime ago. I have not drawn for any and I would fain hope to get into some way before it is exhausted. I endeavoured what I could to get myself excused from the above commision but it would not do. I must have applied to some merchant who must know me before he would have taken my bills on Hogg and Kinlochs.* I have wrote them that I have no occassion for money here but that as I am going to the northward I hope they will honour any draught I may send from thence—you may be sure I shall be sparing in this, and I think if matters are accomadated betwixt England and the Colonies I shall have no occassion for any. You can send the carpet to Glasgow for Savannah directed to Robert Mackay Esq<sup>re</sup>, Augusta, to the care of Thomas Netherclift* Esq<sup>re</sup>, Savannah, Georgia; the paper mentioned in the memorandum must be let alone, it cannot be sent.

As I am to ride through several towns I shall have often an opportunity of writing you. My respects to the Selby family, my duty to our Dear Mother, my kindest affection to yourself and am ever yours

Will$^m$ Mylne

I had almost forgot to wish you all a happy new year. May we live to see one another established in some setled state more at our ease than we have been this long time past. I have been obliged to stay in this town for a fortnight waiting for my trunk—this I intend to leave at M$^r$ Hatfields to be sent by sea after I have got some place to stay at. It is very dear living here and suits not me, therefore as my things are directed to his care I shall set out to morrow without waiting any longer for their coming.

---

It is evident that William wished to avoid carrying much currency on his overland journey and had therefore given it to Robert Mackay in exchange for the "order" that Ogilvey would either pay in cash at Charleston or convert into bills of exchange payable in London, Edinburgh, or as it transpired, New York. The transaction indicates that Mackay carried on his trade in the money of South Carolina and not that of Georgia. After the value of the Carolinian pound had fallen heavily relative to sterling in the early years of the century, the strength of South Carolina's exports had sustained its currency at a steady value from 1730 onward of about £7 local currency to £1 sterling. Internal business in the colony was greatly helped by the issue of paper currency, and South Carolina notes also circulated widely in Georgia. Georgia's own currency, though valued nearly at par with sterling, had not the standing of South Carolina's, which was therefore used for much of Georgia's commerce.

William could obtain money from Scotland during his residence in the colonies by bills of exchange. These would be drawn (i.e., issued) by a banker or merchant in Scotland for a sum of money paid in by Anne; on presentation of the bill to the drawer's agent or "correspondent" in some colonial city the equivalent in local money (or in a further bill to obtain cash in some other place) would be paid to William. The correspondent either held money belonging to the drawer or was willing to give him credit. He would normally be informed in advance by the drawer that the bill had been drawn, and the difficulty that Anne seems to have experienced in sending £50 to William was presumably due to his failure to say where and from whom he would seek to cash her bill. She therefore sent a "letter of credit," which probably granted credit for £50 with the bankers Hogg and Kinloch to William himself and was payable by any merchant or banker who was satisfied as to William's identity and with the security of Hogg and Kinloch's letter.

---

To William Mylne Esq[re.]
    at Powderhall near Edinburgh

                              Augusta, 20th April 1775

Dear Sir

As I had not the pleasure of hearing from you after you got to Charlestown, I'm uncertain whether you was paid my draft on M[r] Ogilvey; and as he has since gone to Great Brittan without writing me any thing on the subject, am in some doubts about that matter; but I hope you was not disapointed. I am but a few days returned from Sav[a] where I was detained upwards of ten weeks in geting our Indian accounts passed.[18] They are finished, but heavy deductions are made from them, near 30 p cent. However if we can get the ballance still due, 'twill make us all easy. American affairs are much the same as when you left us, not less violent I assure you; but the ffolks on your side the water, we are in hopes, will make all matters easy, we impatiently wait for the February and March mails from which we hope to find something definitive resolved on by Parliament. If you yield an inch in this matter, adieu to Great Brittans power over America.

M[r] Gordon and M[r] Brown are both at New Richmond where they plant indigo and if the season proves favourable they will

---

18. Evidently the accounts to support a claim for payment by the government of debts due to him by the Creeks and Cherokee, under the Ceded Lands agreement. The *Georgia Gazette* published on December 28, 1774, a call for claims to be presented on Tuesdays from January to May 1775 at the council chamber in Savannah.

make a tolerable cropt. Mʳ Gordon has been very sick for months past which has reduced him much—he is now on the mending hand. I hope you still continue in the thoughts of returning here to become a settler among us, in which case I must begg of you to bring or send over an house carpenter, Waiscoat is so exceedingly slow that there is no patience with him, 'tho' otherwise a good man. I wou'd not have one of your very fine workmen, any person that understood the business in the coarsest way wou'd answer my purpose—and I wou'd agree to give him 30 to £40 sterling a year and pay his passage out. In case such a man as I want comes your way, youll oblige me greatly in securing him for me & I will thankfully repay any expence you may be at in the matter.

Mrs Mackay and Mʳˢ Williams are both well and desire their compᵗˢ to you. Bob [19] too is quite hearty and enquires after Mungo. Mʳˢ Williams has been a widow since the 9ᵗʰ last January. We all intend a visit to Rhode Island about the first of June, provided they don't come to blows in Boston, shou'd this happen it will disapoint us of a jaunt which our hearts are much set on at present. There is nothing new in this part the country—the Indians are all quiet, and the Ceded Lands are selling fast.

I have another commission to trouble you with & that is youll bring me a good gold watch of abt. twenty guineas value. I think a good one may be got for this sum or a little more—but this Ill leave to your mannagement, also a seal with the letters $R \, M$ in a cypher not very large—I begg you'll excuse my giving you so much trouble, and if ever we meet I'll endeavour to make it up in some way or other. I am truly,
   Dear Sir,
    Your most obedᵗ· servᵗ·
     Robert Mackay

The inclosed letters I took out of the Savannah post office & returns them agreeable to your direction.

---

19. Robert Mackay II.

# Chapter 4

## CHARLESTOWN TO NEW YORK

To
  Miss Ann Mylne
   at M$^r$ Robert Selby's, Baillie Fyfe's Closs,
    Edinburgh, North Britain

New York 1$^{st.}$ March 1775

My Dearest Nanny

I wrote you from Charlestown to inform you I had commenced that long journey I had plan[n]ed in the back country—I left that town the fifth of Jan$^y$ last, crossed Cooper River* with my horse and poor Mungo. I had rode about twenty miles when the road parted in two, I took out a map I had of this province to examine which to take, the crumpling of the paper stratled [sic] the horse, who leaped fairly out below me. After I got up I saw him galloping through the woods; at a mile's distance he came out again to the road, a traveller catched him and brought him back. My saddle bags in his career had come off[f], I now thought I should be obliged to return as the few shirts I had were there. I went into the woods, tracing the tract he had taken as near as I could, by the greatest good fortune after an hours search I found them. I now proceeded on my journey to Georgetown,* which I reached in two days and a half, most of the land all the way very indifferent, being pine barren except in some places where there were indigo plantations.

I crossed the ferry to Georgetown, and here to my great sorrow it was I lost my poor dog. A man had come over in the same boat with two horses, who had travelled all that day with me, he went

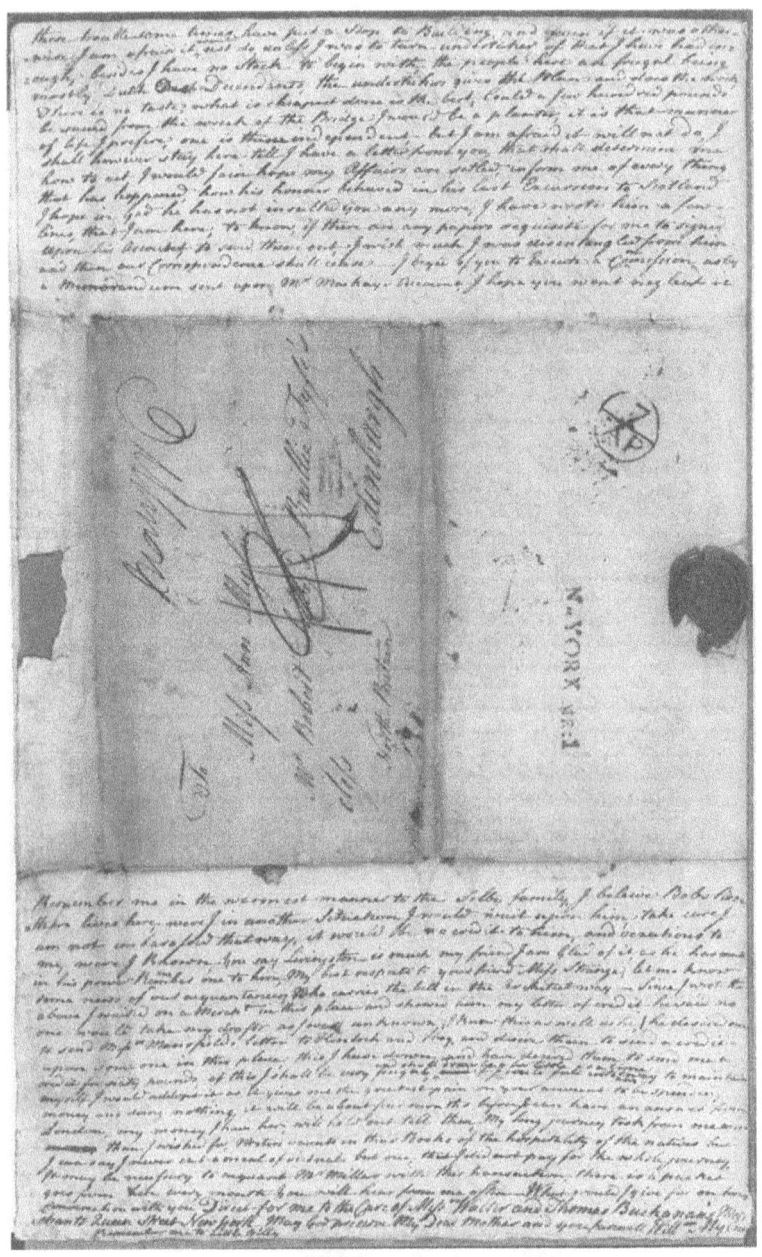

Portion of Mylne's March 1, 1775, letter to his sister Anne.
Courtesy of Captain W. R. J. Mylne.

by the back of the town, I to an inn as I wanted to see the place. I imagine Mungo had followed him thinking me in company. When I missed him, I went to the ferry where I found the negroes who had brought us over, they told me the dog had come back and that when he could not find me he run they knew not where. I offered a reward for finding him but all would not do. The sheriff of the place happened to be in the house and seeing me so uneasy promised to take care of him in case he could come across him at any time, for I had pointed out his virtues as the man did his ass in the S——l journey.[1]

Georgetown is pretily situate at the junction of several navigable rivers, it carries on a considerable trade having many great plantations for rice and indigo at its back. Many of the houses command fine prospects, there may be about 500 houses in it, several considerable merchants resides here. Thinking to overtake the man who I now imagined Mungo had followed (for he had told me that he was to go the same road) I set out; just as I was on horseback a gentleman came up and told [me] a Doctor Gibb* wanted much to see me, I asked how the doctor knew I was in the place, he said it was from him he had learned it, for he had seen me in Charlestown and knew me again. He said the doctor was a school fellow of mine and wished much to see me. I could not think of dismounting, expecting to overtake the man whom Mungo had followed. I beged excuses and set of[f], I understood afterwards that this Doctor Gibb was one of the most considerable men in the town, had a large plantation with many negroes and the best practice of any in his proffesion in these parts, but who he could be I could never recollect. I pushed on to Black River* where as it was a ferry I hoped to get intelligence. No such person had passed; if the man stole him, he had certainly taken another road on purpose. I now gave him over as lost and went on my journey with a heaveness about me I had not felt for some time before.

My road for two days was very disagreable through swamps, I

1. William's long journeys with only Mungo for companion bear a marked resemblance to those of the German, in Laurence Sterne's *A Sentimental Journey* (1768), who made a pilgrimage with only his ass to the shrine of Saint Iago in Spain. Weeping over the ass's death when nearing home, he praised him as an almost human friend.

crossed several rivers in flats.² I came at last to the boundary house where the line runs that divides the south and north provinces. I had intended to lodge there all night, the family were from home, I took possesion of a large hall in which was a good fire and some negro servants. When they came back, entered the Master, a decrepid wretch, I asked for lodging; he said I was welcome for myself but would have nothing to do with my horse, I told him my horse was what I minded more than myself. Nothing would do, I could not help saying some severe things upon his want of hospitality, I got up and went to the stable when I found my poor creature turned out, I was within little of returning to abuse the scoundrel. Although it was near night I set out, the moon was clear, I rode about 10 miles, I tried to make a fire but everything was so wet with the frost rind I could not; at some distance I found a path that led to a house, I went there, the people were a bed but got up and let me in. They were poor and had but one bed, I laid myself before the fire and slept like a top. The landlord next morning was going to Brunswick* and we set out together.

    Brunswick is pleasantly situate near the mouth of Cape Fear River,* it is a poor place and irregular built. They have a large church without a parson and a house which was once the residence of the Governor. I set out for Wilmington,* which is at the distance of 17 miles further up the river. I was told to keep to the plainest road, at 10 miles the road seperated in two, I took the broadest. There was mile posts upon it, I rode to the 20th, when I found I was wrong. I turned of[f] through the woods to catch the other, I wandered about till eleven a clock at night when I got upon a path that led to an old field where was a cabbin wanting the roof, into it I put my horse, and having secured the door I laid me down to sleep. It would not do, it was a strong frost and exceeding cold. At day break I wandered about in search of a road, often obliged to get of[f] my horse and lead through swamps; after near five hours, I got to the same road I had left the night before, I rode down it till I came to the 15 mile post, then struck again into the woods to find the other, I came to a path that led to a house where I was told I had been twelve mile from the place I intended to go to. I got to a tavern where I refreshed, I crossed tow [two]

---

2. Wide flat-bottomed boats or rafts used as ferries.

branches of Cape Fear River to get to Wilmington. Upon the northernmost stands this town, it is a place of considerable trade but from its situation must be disagreable in summer, it stands on a bed of sand inclosed every way with high sandy grounds. It is chiefly composed of two streets crossing each other, the one running parralel to the River. The market place, with the Town House above, stands in the place where the two streets meet; this was a capital error as it interrupts the prospect every way. What is mostly exported from this place is tar and turpentine, staves and lumber, indeed the country I had rode through is fit for nothing else being mostly pine trees. They have convenient wharfs to load the ships, their are flats[3] some miles below the town from which they can only take in part of their loading till they pass them, the rest being sent down in boats. I was told the tide flows 100 miles above this place, where there is a fine country, well setled, many of our country people is there, amongst the rest Flora M<sup>c</sup>Donald* with her husband Barrisdale.*

I forgot to mention I saw Murray* of Philliphaugh at the tavern I came to after my severe nights quarters, he was on his way to Georgia to setle there, having sold his interest in this province; he was well dressed and well attended but I understood was much hated on account of his pride.

After a stay of two days to rest my horse I set out for Newburn* which I reached in three more. In going into the town I was much surprised at the sight of a very fine house, I found it was the Governors. It was by far the largest and most elegant I had seen in America, it is built upon the plan of Buckingham House* with offices joined to it by a collonade; it is really handsome and well proportioned, it is of brick and cost about £15 000 sterling. By accident I fell in company with the man who was both Architect and superintended the work,[4] he was brought over by Governor Tryon.* In conversation I turned upon the house which I much commended. It is natural for people whose hobby horse is flattered to open their hearts, I appeared much surprised that a man of his merit should lived [*sic*] buried in a small town, he said it was his case that he had married there, that he had effects in land

3. Shoals or mudflats.
4. John Hawks.*

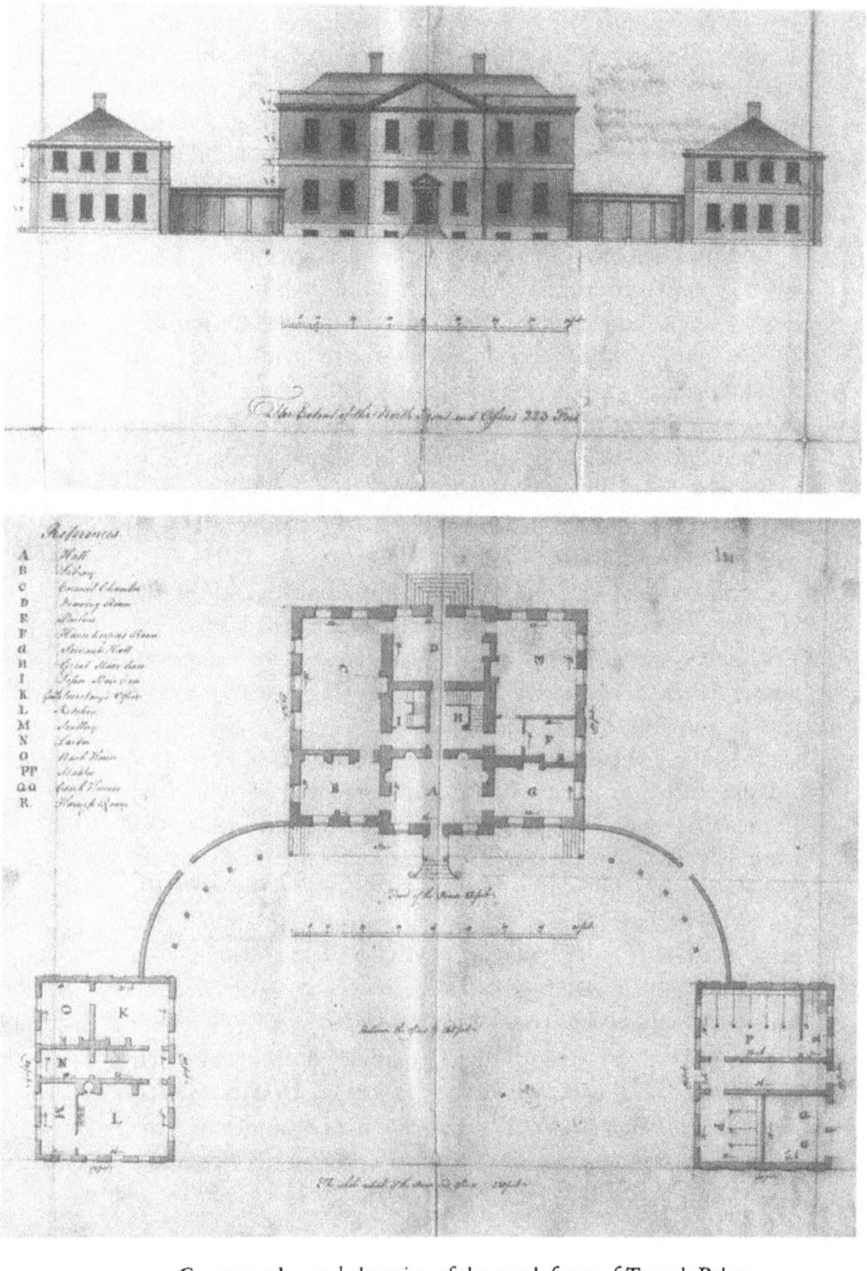

Contract plan and elevation of the north front of Tryon's Palace.
British Public Record Office, CO 5/300.

etc. which he could not turn into money, that Governor Tryon when he went to the government of New York caused him move there, that he staid there nine weeks without any encouragement. I thought all this bad heartning to me.

Newburn is pleasantly situate at the junction of two rivers the Neuse* and the Trent,* it is much like Charlestown with regard to situation but has the advantage in not having those nasty marshes nigh it which is so prejudicial to the health of the inhabitants of the other. Here is the seat of Government for North Carolina. In going down the river are marshes which obliges vessels only to take in a part of their cargo at the town, the rest being sent after them in boats. The exports from this are much the same with Wilmington, tar, pitch, turpentine, with provisions for the West Indies, staves and lumber.

I left New Newburn [sic] and to avoid a large ferry I rode up the country for Tarrborough,* I crossed Neuse River, from this in two days travelling I passed much good land and many plantations; much indian corn is raised here, there is likewise made tarr and turpentine. In several little rivers were many schooners loading corn for New England and the West Indies. I crossed the River Tarr* on a long wooden bridge at the end of which stands the town of Tarrborough, it is a poor dirty place, every step a horse makes he is up to the knees, it was so at this time being rainy weather for some days before. In tow days more I reached Roanoke River.* The day before I had taken up my quarters at a tavern on the road about 20 miles short of it. A Virginian who came up persuaded me to go along, as it was early I agreed, he had a friend he said at some distance where we could lodge; when we got there no such person was to be found. We set out in search of a lodging from some of the neighgbouring [sic] planters, the first we got to was a widows who could afford nothing for our horses, we rode on and got to a plantation of one Coll. Mumford's,* there was no one there but an overseer and his wife with some negroes, they had but one bed, the man was sick. Here we staid all night lying on the floor with a good fire at our feet and our saddles for a pillow.

Next morning we crossed Roanoke, this is a fine river with much good land on its banks which is subject to be overflowed in heavy rains. A town called Hallifax* stands about 8 mile higher up at which a good deall of business is done. Here I parted with the Virginian, I next crossed the Meherin, a small river half a mile from which is the line that divides the provinces of North Carolina and Virginia. I lodged here at a widows plantation, who I so effectually co[a]xed by stories of my travells that both myself and horse were well taken care of. Next morning she insisted for me to stay breakfast, I told her my business was express but that I would call as I came back, I began to think she harboured a favourable opinion of me not from my pretty person but from the strange stories I told. *Avasthauling,*[5] *no matrimony.* She had a good plantation 7 or 8 stout negroes and 4 children, she was about thirty, in her person neat and clean, well looked. I proceeded and crossed the River Ottoway* on a wooden bridge at a place called Southampton Courthouse.* Here I saw some of the remains of an Indian nation called the Ottoways, they are now dwindled to about fifty and are setled nigh this place. The imoderate use of rum has been the occassion of it, one of their women not long ago was drunk and no one nigh her, she tumbled into the fire and was burnt to death.

In two days travelling I came to Williamsburgh* the capital of Virginia, it stands 4 miles from James River.* This is a noble river, where I crossed it it was three miles and a half broad. Williamsburgh stands in a level country and consists of three streets running parralel to each other, the principal one in the middle and is near a mile long, at one end stands the Capitol facing down the street, as the College[6] does at the other. The Capitol is a large building with a portico of two stories. Upon the top is a cupola too small in proportion to the building. My landlord having procured the keys we went together—in the Hall stands the statue of Lord Botetourt* their late Governor for whose memory the people of the province have a great regard, it stands on a pedistal inclosed with iron rails, it is dressed in robes such as the Peers[7] wears, with a wig tied behind and stiff curls. I who had seen so many statues dressed in the Roman and Grecian manner was shocked at the want of taste, I suppose the sculpture [*sic*] had dressed it

---

5. A word apparently coined by William. Possibly referring to the hauling in of sails.
6. College of William and Mary.*
7. The noblemen in the upper house of the British Parliament.

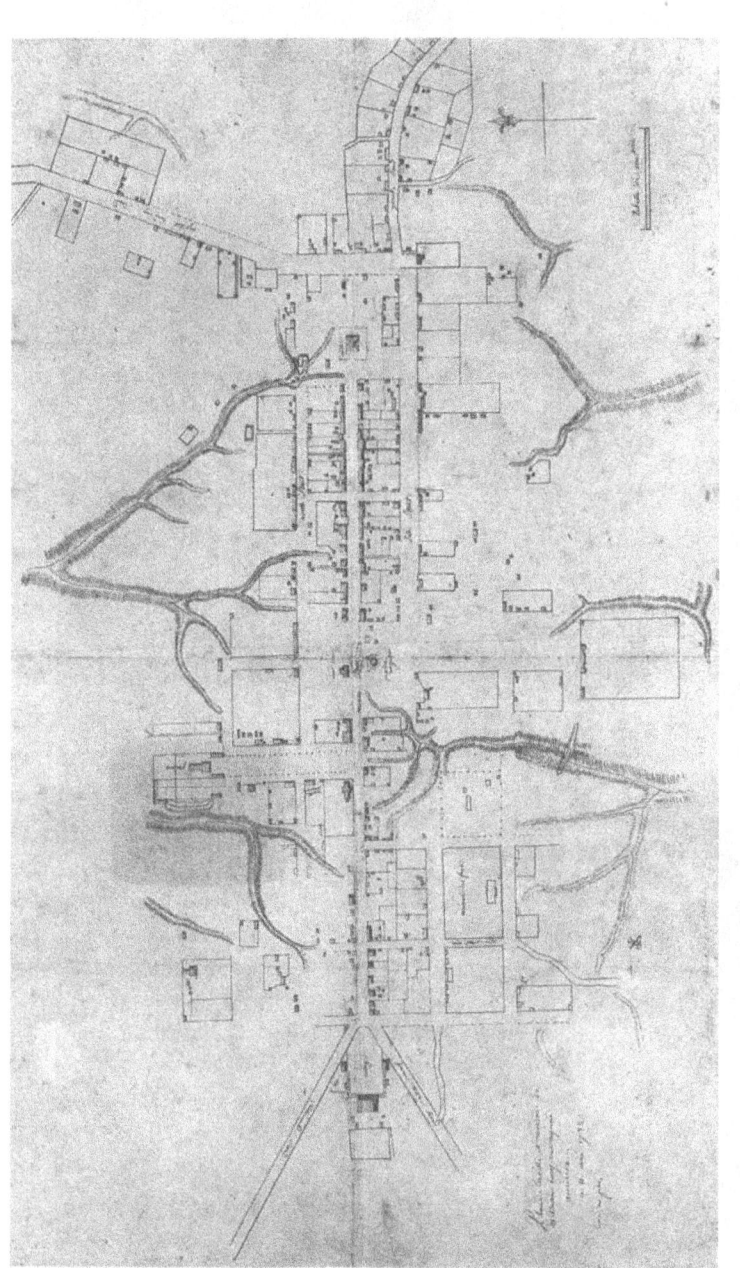

"The Frenchman's Map" of Williamsburgh, Va., 1782. Earl Gregg Swem Library, The College of William and Mary, Williamsburg. Photograph courtesy of Colonial Williamsburg Foundation.

Statue of Lord Botetourt, sculpted by Richard Hayward.
The College of William and Mary.

The Governor's Palace, Williamsburg, Va., circa 1740.
Detail from an engraving in the Bodleian Library, Oxford University.
Photograph courtesy of Colonial Williamsburg Foundation.

so to please his employers; for a man in the company at the house when I returned observed it was a fine statue for it was highly polished. In the lower part of the building was the Hall; the Assembly Room seated as the House of Commons is in England, with a Chair for the Speaker at one end; the Court where causes are tried. Above stairs are the Council Room, several Comittee Rooms, rooms for the Grand and Petit Juries. In the Council Room is a library mostly consisting of law books, it is convenient for the business required. The College is a large building divided into several classes for the students on the lower floor with a chapel where prayers are read evening and morning; the second and third floors consist in appartments for the masters and students.

    The principal street in this town is almost a level from one end to the other, their are several neat houses in it although none grand; upon one side at a little distance is the Governor's house with an area before it. It seems to me as if additions had been made from time to time, as the province had encreased.

    Williamsburgh will never be a large town, it stands so far of[f] the river. Merchants and planters live on the banks of rivers where vessels comes to their doors. Their is a town about 50 miles of[f],

Norfolk,* which from its situation is become a large trading place, standing on James River farther down. Lord Dunmore* was gone there with four Shawnese chiefs he had brought as hostages from his late expedition; he had a new born daughter christned the other day by the name of Virginia and gave a ball on the occassion, it was the Queens Birthday. He is not liked in his government—the late Governor I imagine was your old crony Betsey Tomson's father.[8]

I staid two days in Williamsburgh and then set out for Maryland. To avoid crossing the Great Bay of Chesepeak* which is a ferry of 21 miles I rode up the country, I crossed several rivers amongst which were Potowmack* and Rappahanock. I must observe that most parts of Virginia is well cultivate and well peopled. The inhabitants have in a great measure given over the culture of tobbaco and raise wheat which is bought from them by the merchants of Pensilvania, who convert it into flour for the West India and other markets. Great numbers of Scotch are setled in these parts both as merchants and planters.

After 5 days ride I got to Annapolis,* this is a pleasant situate town, yet a new one called Baltimore* further up the country carries away the greatest part of the trade. It is built upon no regular plan, the streets many of them being winding. They are building a State house which is very large and of brick, it is but just covered in, has a cupola on it not finished. It is designed for the meetings of the Assembly, Courts of justice, councils, etc. They have already been four years in building and I imagine it will take as much more to finish it. The people of Maryland like those of Virginia are leaving the culture of tobacco for that of wheat.

After a days stay I set out for Pensilvania, I passed through Baltimore which is new, it has encreased in a few years from a few houses to a considerable town, much larger than Annapolis; the streets are not as yet paved, and the great concourse of waggons have cut the ground every where so that in many places a horse goes to the belly. At some distance are considerable iron works and many Dutch are settled here.

---

8. This seems mistaken. Botetourt was the late governor, and the only recent governor who had a daughter named Elizabeth (or Betsey) was Robert Dinwiddie. She died unmarried in 1773. Betsey Tomson cannot be identified.

I had fallen in with a man and wife the day before, they were young and fond of each other, they had a child seven months old, dont you think it strange for women to travell long journeys a horse back with a child in their arms, it is common in this part of the world. I had taken a great liking to the child as it never cried, although it was frost and snow, it was always merry and laughing when we got to the side of a large fire. They carried it time about, and once handing from one to the other, the father missed his hold and the poor thing fell to the ground, his horse went right over it. I who have a heart as soft as butter for the weak and helpless jumpt of[f] my horse, when I came to it I was almost afraid to touch it lest it had been killed. I took it up, it looked at me and fell a crying, I felt for the poor mother who sat on her horse quite stupid, the father was little better. I examined its legs and arms and found all safe. I had taken a great liking to this couple, they were young, handsome and fond of one another without fulsomeness, they seemed in easy circumstances; as I had done them some little services, the husband when crossing Susquehana River* in the flat came up, took me in his arms and beggd I would go and stay eight days at his house. I refused him. We were to part on the opposite side. When I went to bid his wife farewell by a friendly shack {sic} of the hand he insisted I should salute her; this done, we went different roads. It is amazing the connection that some people forms almost instantly which is not to be done by others in a whole lifetime; we had travelled two days together and although it was a hard frost and snowed almost constantly we were as merry as crickets, we made good way too for we travelled near 80 miles.

In a few days I came to Philadelphia, in my way I passed through many pleasant villages in a fine cultivate country. Indeed here a man travells as much at his ease as in England, there being good inns and good beds, proper accomadations for ones horse, a great difference betwixt this and to the southward where I have road thirty miles without seeing a house. Through the northern parts of Virginia and along Maryland the planters in general live much at their ease having good estates and good houses, but in Pensilvania one is as it were in the best parts in England, it is a fine country if the people would be good.

Philadelphia is by far the finest laid out town I have ever yet been in. The streets cut one another at right angles; it is pleasently

View of Philadelphia Market in 1800. Engraving by W. Birch & Son. Historical Society of Pennsylvania.

situate on the River Delaware,* where are many large wharfs to which vessels of any size can ly. They are indebted for this plan to their great founder Will^m Penn.* Although the town is large, one half of the plan is not yet compleated, it is inrended to go as far as a river called Schuyl Kill* which is at the distance of two miles from the Delaware. There is a want of variety, a likeness runs through every street in the town, few spires are to be seen. They have the finest market in the world, the roof stands upon brick arches, the stalls are on each side with a walk in the middle; it is at least half a mile long; there is plenty of every kind of meat, fish and fowl, sold very reasonable, this is one of the greatest trading places in America. I sold my horse to a man that had travelled the last days journey with me, I made some profit upon him. I parted from him with great reluctance, he was an old friend that had kept me company in my solitude in the back woods, he had carried me many thousand miles. One of our best English horses could never have undergone the fatigue of this journey.

I left Philadelphia after two days stay and set out in a passage boat for Bordentown* 30 miles distant, there were many passengers, we run it in four hours. We staid at this village all the rest of the day and night, next morning we got into waggons, ten in each, we travelled 40 miles to South Amboy,* here we lodged. Next morning we embarked in the stage boat for this place, it was evening when we arrived, I lodged in a tavern, next morning I took private lodgings. Thus I put an end to a long journey, tho' an agreable one, many people wonders how I could venture it by myself, but I am never subject to fear.

I wrote all this from my memory for I durst not keep a journal, in many places they talked of spies being out, I was afraid I might be taken for one, if a journal had been found I should have been tarred and feathered, an honour the Mobility* sometimes confers on those they apprehend are friends to Government. As to politicks I think most of the people are mad, in South and North Carolina, Virginia, Maryland, they muster and are every where learning the excercise as if they were going to be attacked. In South Carolina they have several companies in uniforms, very gay, being scarlet faced with black velvet, their artillery company is blue faced with scarlet, gold buttons holes. They were raising two companys of light horse when I came away. At Williamsburg their uniform is blue faced with buff. In the back parts the{y} have several companies whose excercise is shooting with rifled guns at a dollar fixed to a tree at the distance of 120 paces, these are the most dangerous, being accustomed to fighting amongst the trees with the Indians they are very dextorous, I have seen one of them take of{f} the head of a hawk at the distance of a hundred yards with a single bullet. In Maryland they muster every where, I could get no sleep for some time at Annapolis for the noise of their drums and fifes excercising in an old playhouse closs by where I lodged, they make use of the night as well as the day. In Pensilvania and this province there is no mustering. This people are divided in two parties, how these sons of Mars will behave in case they come to blows I cannot say, but am of opinion with an old Irishman whom I met on the road as we past a muster field (he was one of the Hearts of Steel* and was obliged to leave his country about that affair) that one third would run away, one third be killed, the other hanged. Trade is in a manner stoped, the other day a ship was sent back that had brought out goods from England, another that lies here will share the same fate.

I have wrote a long letter, but I could have added twice as much had there been room. I must say something about my own situation. I have been near a fortnight in this place, as far as I can judge I have not any prospect of being employed as an architect, these troublesome times have put a stop to building, and even if it was otherwise I am afraid it would not do unless I was to turn undertaker,[9] of that I have had enough. Besides I have no stock to begin with. The people here are frugal being mostly Dutch decendants, the undertakers gives the plan and does the work. There is no taste; what is cheapest done is the best. Could a few hundred pounds be saved from the wreck of the bridge I would be a planter, it is that manner of life I prefere, one is thene independent, but I am afraid it will not do. I shall however stay here till I have a letter from you that shall determine me how to act, I would fain hope my affairs are setled. Inform me of every thing that has happened, how his honour behaved in his last excursion to Scotland, I hope in God he has not insulted you any more, I have wrote him a few lines that I am here, to know if there are any papers requisite for me to signed [*sic*] upon his account, to send them out. I wish much I was disentangled from him, and then our correspondence shall cease.

I beged of you to execute a commission as by a memorandum sent upon M$^r$ Mackays account, I hope you wont neglect it. Remember me in the warmest manner to the Selby family, I believe Bobs brother lives here, were I in another situation I would wait upon him. Take care I am not embarassed that way, it would be no credit to him and vexatious to me, were I known. You say Livingston is much my friend, I am glad of it as he has much in his power. Remember me to him. My best respects to your friend Miss Strange, let me know some news of our acquantances; who carries the bill in the architect way.

Since I wrote the above I waited on a merch$^t$ in this place and showed him my letter of credit, he said no one would take my drafts as I was unknown (I knew this as well as he), he desired me to send Mess$^{rs}$ Mansfields letter to Kinloch and Hog, and desire them to send a credit upon someone in this place, this I have down

---

9. Building contractot as distinct from architect. Mylne was architect and "undertaker" in the Edinburgh bridge project.

[sic] and have desired them to send me a credit for sixty pounds. Of this I shall be very frugal and shall draw but for little at a time, if I could fall into any way to maintain myself I would addopt it as it gives me the greatest pain on your account to be spending money and doing nothing. It will be about four months before I can have an answer from London, my money I have here will hold out till then. My long journey took from me more than I wished for. Writers vaunts in their books of the hospitality of the natives but I can say I never eat a meal of victuals but one that I did not pay for the whole journey. It may be necessary to acquant M$^r$ Millar* with this transaction. There is a packet goes from here every month, you will hear from me often. What would I give for an hours conversation with you.

Direct for me to the care of Mess$^{rs}$ Walter and Thomas Buchanan's,* Merchants, Queen Street New York. May God preserve my Dear Mother and you. Farewell

Will$^m$ Mylne

Remember me to Little Willy

[on verso] Write immediatly for I long to hear from you.

## Chapter 5

## RETURN TO BRITAIN AND END OF STORY

William returned to London in September 1775.

M<sup>r</sup> William Mylne
M<sup>r</sup> Molhorst,[1] Cabinet maker
Little tower hill
   London

Edin<sup>r</sup> October 3 1775

Welcome my Dearest Willy—most sincerely welcome, your arrival has removed every disagreable fear the horrid situation of affairs in America kept me in on your account. —But good God how am I astonished at your silence on my late important change of life, a long and distinct account of which I wrote the begining of May and went in the June packet. —O my Dear Willy rejoice with me in that change, that at least one of your troubles is removed, in no longer being distracted with my future provision; and that I am placed under the most generous and affectionate of protectors.

I write this half an hour after the receipt of yours so that I have had no time for the latest information. —Livingston I met in the street eight days ago. The result of the squire[2] visit here in August was a promise from Lord Elliock, to pronounce his determina-

---

1. Unidentified.
2. Robert Mylne, who was in Edinburgh August 14–21 and August 30–September 7.

tion before the end of September, that and Oct' is gone, and yet nothing is done. He was most liberal in his promises of being very much your friend—but heaven defend me from such an indolent, unsteady man.

Whatever little money came into Livingston's hand, he told me, had been given to John Nicoll,* whose account is considerable reduced. All here remain (except myself) just as you left them. Tho I long most earnestly to see you, I make you sole judge of how your [sic] to act. I would earnestly wish you were with my mother in these long nights. Willy is at the Latin and is a fine boy. But my mother will not allow him to call of me [sic], because *I am too grand*—O my dr Willy, fall not into this weak minded error, only consider me still your bosom friend—the same sympathising affectionate sister. Sir John[3] is prepared to receive you, as your most sincere friend as [sic] is most seriously interested in your welfare.

If money is required draw upon me directly, do not I intreat you scruple about this. As I am pretty sure that there is nothing done by Elliok, I shall keep your arrival a secret from all but our own mother, who from your last I prepard to expect you. I shall wait impatiently for your next. God bless you and preserve you,
     prays
      your sister Anne Gordon

Direct Lady Gordon, St Andrews Square, Edin'·

Mrs & Miss Strange are here, but set out on Monday for France. They have given up house in London, are to settle in Paris. Once more God bless you. The Selbys are well, the whole girls are at a Yorkshire boarding school.

Remember I await your orders and till then am silent.

---

3. Sir John Gordon.*

To
Mr. Will^m Mylne
Mr. Molhorst, Cabinet Maker
Little tower
      Hill    London

                                  Edin^r
                          thursday 16 of Nov^b

... Livingston I sent a note to, to know if he had received any letter from you—his answer was that he had—and was just going to wait on Lord Elliok to know if he required your presence perhaps this may rouse him. At all events let me beg of you to come down. Whatever plan you may have, if it is unconected with London, why would you stay an hour where your expence, however sober, is reducing your ready money still lower. For the same reason let me conjure you to give up the thoughts of taking a room[4]; seting aside the odd apearance it would have, why would you grieve your mother by doing so? The reason you give is I allow a most feeling one, but as you come to settle maters, you apear here in the honourable light of relieving the Bashaw, which in a letter of his to you (which you missed, and was returned by Mr. Mackay to me) he says he is left to wind up this troublesome business alone.

    Besides my dearest Willy you can at Powder Hall digest & settle any future plan of operations; if any money will be got of this cursed affair, you can think how to turn it—a desperate disease requires a desperate remedy, something must be done or imediate want will insue. ...

    ... By this post you probably will get Livingston answer; at all events come down; this house[5] and its owners are equally at your command, we have decent ease, now and then a little show. ...

    ... God bless you—do put your things on board of a London ship, & take out a ticket in the fly, & come down—and make happy

                                    your affectionate sister
                                          Anne Gordon.

---

4. William must have suggested renting a lodging instead of staying at Powderhall.
5. Sir John and Lady Gordon's house in Saint Andrew's Square, Edinburgh.

Anne was married, probably early in April 1775, to Sir John Gordon, Baronet, of Earlstone in Galloway, a district in the southwest of Scotland. Anne had only about £200 to offer him as dowry, and half of that was on loan to William—money that she insisted she could not recall until his financial difficulties were resolved. Clearly the family properties at Powderhall and elsewhere were going to pass to Mrs. Mylne's sons, and probably the majority to Robert. Sir John, however, was unworried as long as Anne consented to live on his own modest income. He was nearly fifty years old and a military captain on half pay (that is, retired), a gentleman who wished to settle quietly, but with dignity, in Edinburgh. Doubtless Anne made him an ideal wife, with the liveliness of mind that shows in her few surviving letters, her fine looks,[6] and the experience of caring for her mother, brother, and nephew, and overseeing one or two servants.

The wedding took place in the dining room at Powderhall. Without nuptial feasting, the couple left immediately for a stay of several weeks with friends of Anne's at Durham, returning only when the house they had rented in Saint Andrew's Square in Edinburgh's New Town was ready for occupation. This was necessary because Anne thought Powderhall unfit for entertaining her husband's relatives. One month after her marriage she wrote to William a long description of her circumstances before she received Sir John's unexpected offer, of her acceptance when the offer came, and her arrangements for the wedding; but the letter never reached him and when she discovered this she wrote it all again in her letter of November 16, 1775, quoted above.

Sir John and Lady Gordon had no children. From 1780 onward they lived at Number 2, Thistle Court, Edinburgh, a small court near Saint Andrew's Square. Sir John carried on some correspondence with William for a few years and clearly respected him. When differences arose between his wife and other Mylnes, chiefly Robert but also her sister Elizabeth Selby,* he seems to have been distressed and he tried, rather unsuccessfully, to act the part of peacemaker. The differences were overcome at least to the extent that Lady Gordon became trustee for Elizabeth's will after her death—probably in 1797—and, on her own death in 1822, left

---

6. A half-length portrait of Lady Gordon, attributed to Romney, was sold in London in 1978.

some money and effects to two of Robert's daughters and arranged for the silver left her by William to be passed, as he had wished, to Robert's son and heir, William Chadwell Mylne.* The latter also owned a portrait of Lady Gordon that he had loaned to her but was returned to him after her death.

Lord Elliock's delay in ruling on William's dispute with the town council, so long bemoaned by Anne, continued until nearly a year after William's return from America. Between December 1771 and September 1772 he had received £2,500 in the form of so-called "loans" from the council; but these were actually payments on account against a total that was yet to be determined. For work he had done that was extra to his original contract, Lord Elliock found that £4,187 was due to him, but against this charged him with £420 of the cost of rebuilding of unsatisfactory walls by the council's overseer after William had left Edinburgh. The council accepted the arbiter's ruling but charged William interest on the loans; their final payment was then £957, paid on April 14, 1777.

William had various debts to settle, but it seems that the money he had received was sufficient. Robert wrote to him in September 1777: "You are out of debt now, or thereabouts," and this included his debts to Robert Selby* and to Anne. William's debt to his brother Robert, which had stood at £765 15s. at the end of 1776, was reduced before mid-1778 by Robert making a "contribution" of £500 to his loss—fulfilment of the intention to which he alluded in his letter to William on March 7, 1774.


In the city of Dublin* there was a piped water supply that caused the town council a considerable amount of trouble from complaints about breakdowns in the supply and about the collection of dues. A large increase in the supply was made possible in the 1770s by taking some of the water that was brought to the city by the Grand Canal of Ireland, built for navigation from the River Shannon to Dublin. While considering their plans for extension in 1776, the council's "pipe water committee" took advice from several people including Thomas Cooley, architect of the new Exchange (now the City Hall) and a former assistant of Robert Mylne; and it was

# RETURN TO BRITAIN AND END OF STORY 83

doubtless Cooley who advised them to write to Robert after their advertisements in Dublin had failed to find a person "skilled in water works" to direct the new works. Robert had been engineer to the New River Company, which supplied the majority of London's water, since 1767, in addition to practicing as an architect; he was therefore likely to find an adequate water engineer for Dublin, if anyone could. Dublin was at that time the second largest city of the British Empire.

Robert's answering letter said that he could send an appropriate man but apparently did not name him. The Dublin town council then asked him to send them the man and offered a salary of £140 per annum and a house to live in. They had made this decision by the middle of October and the man, William, left Edinburgh—how long he had been there is not known—for London at about the middle of November. On arriving in London from America a year earlier, he had lodged with a cabinet maker, keeping his presence a secret, it seems, from his brother; but now he stayed at Robert's house in Arundel Street. He doubtless spent time viewing all of the London waterworks and learning about them from Robert. By January 1777 he was at work in Dublin and on February 3 presented his proposals for a new water main and branches in the southern part of the city—the area south of the River Liffey. On April 7 he produced a plan of supply for the area north of the river. He had already achieved a position of respect and comfort, which drew some teasing remarks from Anne.

---

To Mr William Mylne
        engineer
St Thomas Street No 9 Dublin

Dear Willy                     Edin$^{br}$   March 9   1777
   . . . I am extremly happy to find that everything in Dublin pleases you so well, but could not help smiling when I recolected your former philosophick airs to find you now enumerating the comforts of a good bed, and of different people being at your comand—what an honest soul I have been who never denyed all this.

Owr mother has kept her health this winter wonderfully well; indeed I have long observed that she never is so well as when she has the house to herself. . . .

. . . Willy must go to writing and arithmetic we shall see and get the master as good as we can. . . .

. . . in all changes and chances your sincere friend

Ann Gordon.

---

William's employment in Dublin lasted thirteen years, during which the supply of water to private premises was greatly extended and improved, and his direction of the undertaking was praised repeatedly by the council in the warmest terms. Many new lines of supply were laid in the city; most pipes were of elmwood bored to various diameters in William's own workshop, but the largest mains were of cast iron. Contrary to Anne's gentle taunt, William was neither seduced by newfound comforts and authority nor deflected from his simple-minded integrity of purpose. He deliberately ran the risk of losing both his status and livelihood several times in battles with the pipe water committee and council for money and staff for the service. As early as September 1777 he made up his mind to resign, but then, as on various later occasions, he was persuaded to continue. On more than one of these occasions he was allowed some weeks or months of leave to visit friends and family in England and Scotland, and he also liked to visit Buxton Spa for his health. He provided sums of money, which over a number of years totaled about £600, in support of his son Willy, who in the middle 1780s was serving on ships trading in the East.

In a letter to Robert in 1784 William expressed some satisfaction with his personal circumstances, but real enthusiasm only bubbled over when he wrote of practical success in his waterworks.

Robert Mylne Esq^re
New River Head, Islington,
London.

                               Dublin 4^th Oct^r 1784
Dear Brother
... I have no cause to complain either of my health or stomack these some weeks past; the last has been greatly mended by eating great quantitys of ripe fruit, of which I have great plenty in my little garden. . . . It has likewise removed a giddiness in my head, which had greatly hurt my eye sight.

My cock is the cock of all cocks and beats every thing of that kind that was ever applied to water works. It, and the idle time the turncocks have on their hands by its operation, with the aid of whiskey makes them cry Cock a Liralu. . . .

I am now erecting conduits or . . . fountains for supplying the poor with water. . . . The fence of the first one will be knocked down in a few days when I shall send you a description of it and the opinion of the public . . . the people here think I can do anything in water works. . . .

                               Yours ever affectionately,
                                   Will^m Mylne.

---

When William was again ready to resign less than two years later, he showed his frustration with his masters in the committee.

---

Robert Mylne Esq^re
New Riverhead,  Islington
London.

                               Dublin 3^d May   1786
Dear Brother
I was much surprised by your last of the 28^th of April, you would have me act so mean a part in asking for a pension. However poor I may be, I spurned the idea; to have made the proposition to such men as these are, would have hurt me more than the loss of my place.

After giving notice in writing I should resign my appointment . . . I was much sollicited to change my intention. To try them to the utmost, I offered, if they would manfully oppose every encroachment on their works . . . I would stand by them to the last moment. I could get no satisfactory answer, some saying it was in vain to oppose Government, *that is to say they were afraid of their places and pensions.* . . .

. . . they voted me a most honorable testimony of my conduct during the many years I have had the management of the works, with the City Seal to be affixed to it. They voted a piece of plate to be given me value thirty pounds with an inscription on it. . . .

Ever sincerely yours

Will$^m$ Mylne

---

When he wrote Robert his last surviving letter, William was not threatening to resign and his mood had shifted nearer to sorrow than anger.

---

Dublin 4$^{th}$ Jan$^{ry}$ 1789

Dear Brother

. . . Our new works has answered every purpose I could have wished for . . . yet I find it will be at least two years more before they are compleated, God send it was over, for I am heartily sick of business. . . . I have some money that lies in our Treasurer's hands, where it is safe, I wish always to let these people see, that I am not a needy man. I have an old and faithfull servant who has attended me during all my illnesses from time to time, for her I wish to make some small provision, as she is now getting past her labour; this will make me continue longer in my employment than I should wish for, she has lived these ten years with me. . . .

Ever most sincerely   Dear Brother
Yours      Will$^m$ Mylne

---

William never reached his retirement. He died in Dublin in March 1790. Only a very brief abstract of his will survives. It was dated March 6 and proved on June 19, and the two names men-

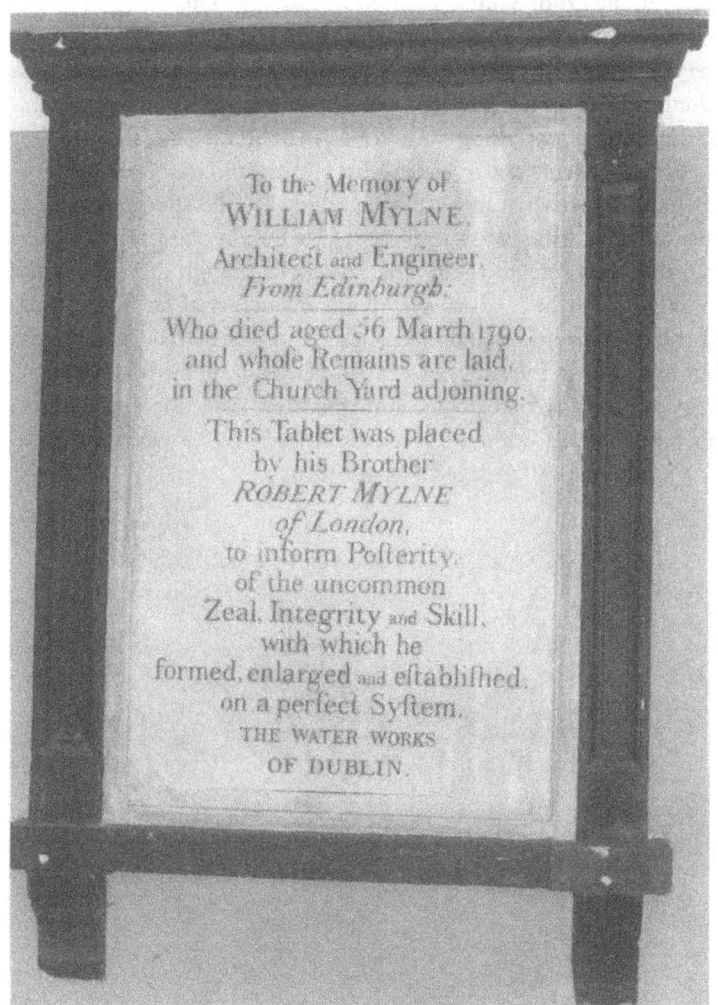

Memorial to William Mylne in St. Cathetine's Church, Dublin.

tioned, presumably as chief legatees, were his brother Robert and nephew, who, as William Chadwell Mylne, was to succeed Robert as engineer to the New River Company. William was buried in the churchyard of Saint Catherine's Church in Dublin and in due course Robert had a fine memorial to him carved and erected in the south aisle of the church. It is still there and well preserved, though the church is now disused. The office, yard, and workshops of the water undertaking were in Saint Catherine's Parish.

William seems not to have written much to Lady Gordon or to Sir John after his first two years in Dublin. But his silver, including the fine salver engraved and presented to him by the city of Dublin in 1786, was sent to them when he died, though intended ultimately for William Chadwell Mylne. A memorial set in the wall of the churchyard of Cramond Kirk, then just outside Edinburgh but now within the suburbs, records the death of Sir John Gordon in 1795, and a second stone commemorates "Anne Mylne, relict of Sir John Gordon," who survived him by twenty-six years and died on October 27, 1822, aged seventy-seven.

# Appendix 1

## WILLIAM MYLNE'S POWER OF ATTORNEY

Abstract of power of attorney from William Mylne to Charles Livingston, September 2, 1773. Held in Register of Deeds at Scottish Record Office.

**POWER OF ATTORNEY MILN TO LIVINGSTON PER D. RAE.**
Know all men by these presents that I William Mylne of the City of Edinburgh Architect have made ordained authorized constituted and appointed and by these presents do make ordain authorize, and constitute and appoint Charles Livingston writer of the City of Edinburgh my true and lawfull attorney ffactor or agent for me and in my name and to my use to ask demand and receive all such sums of money whatsoever which now are or hereafter shall be due and for me and in my name or otherwise to settle sign and adjust any account or accounts touching or concerning the same or any part thereof and if need be to leave the same to reference and to compound and agree for the same or any part thereof and for me and in my name or otherwise to bring any action or actions suit or suits for recovery thereof and of every part thereof and to proceed in such action or actions suit or suits to judgement or execution or otherwise as my said attorney, agent or ffactor shall think fitt or be advised and to discontinue such action . . . if necessary and to have use and take all other lawfull ways and means for the recovery thereof by summons attachment arrest or otherwise as my said attorney . . . shall think fitt and on receipt thereof every or any part thereof acquittances receipts or oyr good and sufficient releases and dicharges for the same for me and in my name . . . and

in my name to let set or demise all my messuages tenements or dwelling houses lands and premises situate and being in the City of Edinburgh and elsewhere . . . leases not to exceed twenty-one years . . . and as I have lately submitted sundry matters in controversy between me and the City of Edinburgh to arbitration, now therefore I do hereby authorize and impower my said attorney . . . to stand to abide and perform all such things as shall be needfull to be done. . . .

Signed and sealed     2 September 1773     William Mylne

## Appendix 2

## CALENDAR OF LETTERS, 1773–1775

The letters listed are those that are known to have been written between William Mylne (WM) and his mother Elizabeth Mylne (EM), his sister Anne (AM), and his brother Robert (RM) between May 1773 and November 1775. Many were not received and lost due to the uncertainties of mail carriage, and there were undoubtedly additional letters of which we have no specific evidence. Some that we know to have been received have since been lost. Most of the letters to William seem to have been directed to Charleston, all those to Anne and Robert to Edinburgh and London, respectively. "Location" below refers to the place where a letter was written or from where it was dispatched. The normal time of carriage for transatlantic mail was from two to three months. (The letters after November 1775 that are quoted in Chapter 5 do not represent a consistent correspondence and are excluded from this calendar. They are scattered fairly randomly through the family correspondence deposited at the Scottish Record Office.)

| LETTER | LOCATION | DATE | NOTES |
|---|---|---|---|
| WM to EM | Edinburgh | May 2, 1773 | Extant |
| WM to AM | London | Aug. 29/Sept. 4 | Extant |
| WM to RM | London | Sept. | Received, now lost. Enclosed power of attorney for solicitor extant. Copy of letter sent to AM received, now lost |

(*continued*)

## APPENDIX 2

| LETTER | LOCATION | DATE | NOTES |
|---|---|---|---|
| AM to WM | Edinburgh | Oct. 1 | Not received |
| AM to WM | Edinburgh | Nov. 1 | Not received |
| AM to WM | Edinburgh | Dec. 1 | Not received |
| WM to RM | Charleston | Dec. | Now lost |
| WM to AM | Charleston | Dec. 21 | Received, now lost |
| AM to WM | Edinburgh | Jan. 1, 1774 | Not received |
| AM to WM | Edinburgh | Feb. 1 | Not received |
| AM to WM | Edinburgh | Mar. 1 | Not received |
| RM to WM | London | Mar. 7 | Received at New Richmond "a few days" before Sept. 1. Copy extant in WM to AM, Oct. 13, 1774 |
| AM to WM | Edinburgh | Apr. 1 | Not received |
| WM to AM | Augusta | Apr. 26 | Now lost |
| AM to WM | Edinburgh | May 17 | Received Aug. 28 Extant |
| WM to AM | Augusta | May 29 | Extant |
| WM to RM | Stephen's Creek | June 26 | Extant |
| AM to WM | Edinburgh | July 28 | Received before Oct. 13, now lost |
| WM to AM | New Richmond | Sept. 1 | Extant |
| WM to RM | New Richmond | Sept? | Now lost |
| WM to AM | New Richmond | Oct. 13 | Extant |
| WM to AM | Charlestown | Jan. 4, 1775 | Extant |
| WM to AM | New York | Mar. 1 | Extant |
| AM to WM | Edinburgh | Early May | Not received |
| AM to WM | Edinburgh | Oct. 3 | Directed to London Extant |
| AM to WM | Edinburgh | Nov. 16 | Directed to London Extant |

# Main Sources

### ABBREVIATIONS

AO     Audit Office papers, Public Record Office, London.
BAL    British Architectural Library, Royal Institute of British Architects, London.
DAB    *The Dictionary of American Biography*. 20 vols. New York and London, 1928–36.
DNB    *The Dictionary of National Biography*. 22 vols. London, 1921–22.
PRO    Public Record Office, London.
SRO    Scottish Record Office, Edinburgh.

### MANUSCRIPT COLLECTIONS

*British Architectural Library,*
*Royal Institute of British Architects, London.*

Mylne Papers, including William Mylne's letters from America, 1773–75, Robert Mylne's diaries, 1762–1810, Robert Mylne's book of family history, ca. 1775, with later additions, and other letters and documents.

*Georgia Historical Society, Savannah.*

Colonial Dames of America Collection, including papers regarding Robert and Mary Mackay.

*Public Record Office, London.*

Loyalist claims and associated correspondence in Audit Office papers of the late eighteenth century.
Treasury series 47/12, concerning Loyalist claims.
Hawks Papers, 5/300 and 310, Colonial Office records.

*Scottish Record Office, Edinburgh.*

Mylne Papers, GD1/51, comprising letters of Anne, Robert, William, and other Mylnes and sundry other papers.
Copies of Robert Mylne's diaries and book of family history.
Registers of births, deaths, and marriages, OPRS and IGI.
Register of deeds, RD2/2/214 (William Mylne's power of attorney).

## MAIN SOURCES

*State of Georgia Archives, Atlanta.*

Surveyor-General's Department.

Records of Commissioners for the Ceded Lands.
Land Grant Books.
Typescript of thesis by M. Cohn, "Thomas Browne: Loyalist."

Department of Natural Resources.

Typescript by M. F. Norwood, "History of the White House Tract," 1975.

*State of South Carolina Archives, Columbia.*

Land Grant Books.

### NEWSPAPERS AND PERIODICALS

*Annual Register* (London)
*Gentleman's Magazine* (London)
*Georgia Gazette*
*London Chronicle*
*South Carolina Gazette*
*South Carolina Historical and Genealogical Magazine*

### OTHER PUBLISHED SOURCES

Alden, J. R. *A History of the American Revolution.* London: Macdonald, 1969.
——— . *John Stuart and the Southern Colonial Frontier.* Ann Arbor: University of Michigan, 1944.
Cashin, Edward J. *The King's Ranger: Thomas Brown and the American Revolution on the Southern Frontier.* Athens: University of Georgia Press, 1989.
Cashin, Edward J., ed. *Colonial Augusta, Key of the Indian Countrey.* Macon, Ga.: Mercer University Press, 1986.
Cashin, Edward J., and Heard Robertson. *Augusta and the American Revolution.* Augusta, Ga.: Richmond County Historical Society, 1975.
Colvin, Howard. *A Biographical Dictionary of British Architects, 1600–1840.* London, 1978.
De Vorsey, Louis. *The Indian Boundary in the Southern Colonies, 1763–1775.* Chapel Hill: University of North Carolina Press, 1961.
Griswold, S. Wesley. *The Boston Tea Party, 16 December 1773.* Brattleboro, Vt.: Stephen Greene Press, 1972.
Harper, Francis. *The Travels of William Bartram.* New Haven: Yale University Press, 1958.
Jackson, Harvey H., and Phinizy Spalding, eds. *Forty Years of Diversity: Essays on Colonial Georgia.* Athens: University of Georgia Press, 1984.
Maitland, William. *History of London.* 2 vols. London, 1760.
Mylne, Robert Scott. *The Master Masons to the Crown of Scotland.* Edinburgh: Scott & Ferguson and Burness & Co., 1893.
Richardson, A. E. *Robert Mylne, Architect and Engineer.* London: Batsford, 1955.

Robertson, Thomas H., and T. Heard. *A Bicentennial Map of Augusta, Georgia, and Surroundings, 1735–1781*. Augusta-Richmond County Bicentennial Committee, Augusta, 1976.

Ruddock, Ted. *Arch Bridges and Their Builders, 1735–1835*. Cambridge: Cambridge University Press, 1979.

———. "The Building of North Bridge, Edinburgh, 1763–1775." *Transactions of the Newcomen Society* 47 (1974–76): 9–33.

Weinreb, Ben, and Christopher Hibbert. *A London Encyclopaedia*. London, 1983.

*Williamson's Directory for the City of Edinburgh, Canongate, Leith, and Suburbs*. Edinburgh, annually from 1773–74 onward.

# Annotated Index

References listed in full in the main sources are listed in the index by a short title. For abbreviations used in these citations, see main sources.

**American Revolution,** 6, 54

**Annapolis,** 72, 75
A plan of Annapolis dated 1718 shows a layout of rectangular blocks, not on a perfect grid and intersected by streets radiating from two open circles, but not a town of winding streets. The layout was the same in a plan of 1781 and is unchanged today. The larger circle is for the State House, spelled Stadt House in the 1770s. The building seen by William was the third Stadt House, designed by Joseph Horatio Anderson, architect, about 1772, and built by Charles Wallace in 1772–79. By a change in his contract, Wallace was allowed to roof it with sheet copper imported from England. The roof, but not the cupola, was completed in the summer of 1774. On September 2, 1775, a hurricane ripped off nearly all the copper, which was damaged beyond repair, and Wallace then framed a steeper roof and covered it with shingles. Further progress was impeded by the war and the building only came into use in 1779. During the eight months in 1783–84 when Annapolis was the national capital the Continental Congress met in the Senate Chamber. In 1785–88 the cupola was replaced by the present wood-framed dome, sixty feet higher, and designed and built by Joseph Clark. In 1902–1905 the building was extended to twice its former volume, but with little alteration of the existing elevations or the original rooms inside. See M. L. Radoff, *The State House of Annapolis* (Annapolis: Maryland Hall of Records Commission, 1972).

**Argyle, Duke of,** 51
John Campbell (1723–1806), fifth duke of Argyll. Inherited the estate and castle of Inveraray in 1770. William Mylne was employed to supervise important alterations, and presumably to design some or all of them, in 1770–72. See I. G. Lindsay and M. Cosh, *Inveraray and the Dukes of Argyll* (Edinburgh University Press, 1973).

**Augusta,** 22–25, 27–29, 33–35, 37–38, 40–49, 53–57, 59, 92
See Cashin, *Colonial Augusta*; Norwood, "History of the White House Tract"; "Fort Augusta," *Georgia Magazine* (Aug.–Sept. 1966): 20–22.

**Baillie, George,** 42, 44

Merchant in Savannah from 1763 and possibly earlier. Granted one thousand acres of land in Saint Paul's Parish on November 1, 1774. Filed a loyalist claim in London for £1,613 and was allowed £300. Great-grandson, on his mother's side, of Robert Mylne (1633–1711). Married but without issue. See AO 12 and 13 at PRO; Grant Book M, State of Georgia Archives; Robert Mylne, family history, BAL.

**Baillie, Willy,** 43–44, 49–50

Nephew of George Baillie and probably son of John Baillie, factor at Penston, between Tranent and Haddington, Scotland. See Robert Mylne, family history, BAL.

**Baltimore,** 72

Port and town in Maryland that grew very rapidly in the second half of the eighteenth century, with a cosmopolitan population of ambitious tradesmen and merchants. In 1787 it had 1,955 houses, 152 stores, and 9 churches. See J. Morse, *An American Geography* (London, 1792).

**Barnard, Edward (d. 1775),** 37, 46–47

Merchant and landowner near Augusta. Lieutenant of His Majesty's Troop of Rangers in Augusta, a force of "provincial regulars." Appointed captain of rangers in the Ceded Lands, 1773. Close friend of Robert and Mary Mackay. See Cashin, *Colonial Augusta*; "Fott James," *Georgia Magazine* (Feb.–Mar. 1968): 19–21.

**Barrisdale (d. 1792),** 65

Allan MacDonald, former factor and tacksman of Kingsburgh on the Isle of Skye, and husband of Flora McDonald. (MacDonalds were so numerous in the islands that a man was often identified by the name of his estate or farm.) William Mylne's use of the name *Barrisdale* may be a corruption of Bernisdale, which was near and possibly within Allan's "tack" (i.e., tenancy) of Kingsburgh. He is unlikely to have been tenant of Barrisdale, which is on the mainland at the head of Loch Hourn. He had served as a lieutenant in the Royalist militia in Scotland in 1745–46. See also **McDonald, Flora**.

**Bedlam,** 15

Colloquial name of the famous lunatic asylum properly called Bethlehem Hospital, "bedlam" has become a synonym for disorder. There was a chilling description of the madness of the inmates in the very successful novel by Henry Mackenzie, *The Man of Feeling* (London, 1771).

**Big Elk,** 38

**Blackfriars Bridge,** 3, 16

The second bridge across the Thames in the City of London. Designed in handsome neoclassical style by Robert Mylne and built under his direction in 1760–70. See Ruddock, *Arch Bridges*.

ANNOTATED INDEX 99

**Black River,** 63
River in South Carolina, flowing into Winyah Bay. A ferry over Black River was first authorized in 1725. Possibly this was the ferry used by William Mylne, and near the line of the present Route 701. See G. C. Rogers, *History of Georgetown County, SC* (Columbia, S.C., 1970).

**Bordentown,** 74
Village in New Jersey on the east bank of the Delaware River, calling point of passage boats.

**Boston,** 6–7, 10, 12, 19–21, 46, 60
First settled in 1630 by English Puritans who were at odds with conventional English society, Boston led the colonies in practical opposition to British control of trade from 1763 onward.

**Boston Tea Party,** 6, 21
The name given to the action of some citizens who tipped into Boston harbor the cargo of the ships sent from London with East India Company tea on December 16, 1773. See Griswold, *The Boston Tea Party*.

**Botetourt, Lord (Norborne Berkeley, Baron de Botetourt [1717–70]),** 68, 70, 72
Appointed governor-general of Virginia in London in 1768, he went immediately to rhe colony, the first governor-general for several decades to reside there. He became very popular and after his death a statue was commissioned by the House of Burgesses. It was carved in London by the English sculptor Richard Hayward, using a wax medallion for a model. It was erected at Williamsburg in 1773 and was unharmed during the Revolution. Later it was mutilated, then partly repaired, and stood outside the college until 1958. It is now in the basement concourse of the library. See *DAB; Statue of Lord Botetourt* (College of William and Mary Library Contributions No. 7. Williamsburg, 1971).

**Boundary house,** 64
A historical marker at the boundary line between North and South Carolina on U.S. 17, which is on or near the route followed by Mylne at this poinr, records the existence of a boundary house in 1775.

**Broad River,** 24, 37, 41–43, 53
A large tributary of the Savannah River on its right bank in upper Georgia. Traverses the northern half of the Ceded Lands.

**Brown, Alexander,** 8, 12
See also **Browns (family)**

**Brown, Thomas** (1750–1825), 36–37, 47, 53–54, 59
Son of Jonas Brown (1719–99), a prosperous merchant, shipowner, and industrialist at Whitby, Yorkshire. Thomas planned a large investment in the

Ceded Lands of Georgia, in partnership with his father and James Gordon; the latter, however, failed to bring any funds to the venture. On arrival in Savannah in 1774 Brown was sworn in as a magistrate and always thereafter took a Loyalist position. At New Richmond on August 2, 1775, he faced nearly one hundred Sons of Liberty alone and refused to join the association against trade with Britain, which he saw as an oath of allegiance to the Continental Congress. He was taken to Augusta, tortured, partly scalped, tarred and feathered, and dragged through the streets. He escaped in a dreadful condition to a Loyalist camp at Ninety-Six in South Carolina and almost immediately became involved in raising Loyalist military forces in the backlands. He formed a policy of creating a backlands force including the Indian tribes to attack the rebels in the rear when British troops arrived on the coast. This policy became the British southern strategy, with Brown, as lieutenant colonel, commanding a corps called the Florida Rangers and sustaining the threat of Indian attack on the rebels throughout the war years. He was a fearless soldier and a skillful motivator of the tribes, for which he was appointed superintendent of Indian affairs of the eastern (and more important) district when John Stuart died in 1779. He commanded the force which reoccupied Augusta for the Crown in 1780 and held "the White House," the old stone-built trading-post that had belonged to Robert Mackay, in a dramatic four-day siege, during which he was seriously wounded. Though he built a new fort—and incidentally resumed the development of his township of Brownsborough—Augusta was taken by the rebels in June 1781. In the postwar years he received large grants of land in the Bahamas and on Saint Vincent and was a highly successful planter. When he filed a Loyalist claim in 1787 for loss of 7,800 acres (including the 5,000 reserved by James Gordon in the Ceded Lands and presumably the area of Brownsborough), he sent medical certificates to London stating that the journey to England would be dangerous to his health, after his recent involvement in shipwreck and severe exposure. Abnormally, his excuse was accepted and his brother, Jonas Brown, Jr., of Kingston-upon-Hull, was permitted to negotiate the claim for him. A sum of £3,500 was allowed and presumably paid to Jonas. See Cashin, *The King's Ranger*; AO 12 and 13 at PRO.

**Browns (family), 40**
Probably the family of Alexander Brown, "cautioner" or guarantor for William Mylne in his bridge contract, 1765, and presumably the Alexander Brown who traded as wine merchant in Craig's Close, Edinburgh, in 1773–78. Related to the Mylnes through Elizabeth, wife of Robert Mylne (1633–1711). See Robert Mylne, family history, BAL; *Williamson's Directory*.

**Brownsborough, 43, 54**

**Bruce, Sir William (ca. 1630–1710), 1**
Scotland's leading architect after the Restoration of the Stuarts in 1660 and

virtual founder of the profession in Scotland. Also held several political offices in the same period. See Colvin, *Biographical Dictionary*.

**Brunswick, 64**
A town on south shore of Cape Fear estuary in North Carolina. Founded to be the provincial capital and was the residence of three royal governors, including Tryon before he moved to New Bern. It was the port of clearance from the Cape Fear estuary. A very large parish church was begun in 1759, but by 1909 only the walls were standing. The town has also virtually disappeared. See A. M. Waddell, *History of New Hanover County and the Lower Cape Fear*, vol. 1 (1909), 10–25.

**Buchanan, Thomas, and Walter Buchanan, 77**
Merchants in New York. Walter was established there before 1763, when Thomas (1744–1815) arrived from Glasgow, where he had studied at the university and trained in the merchant business of his father, who was Walter's cousin. Thomas married Almy Townesend, of a patriot family, and supported non-importation in 1766. Although in later years his political position was more often Loyalist, he avoided confiscation of his property and continued trading, chiefly with Scotland and Jamaica, for thirty years after the Revolution. It has been claimed, but apparently without foundation, that Thomas was the consignee of the cargo of tea that was shipped to New York from London on the *Nancy* in 1773. It has also been said that his partnership with Walter was dissolved in 1772, at variance with William Mylne's use of the partnership's name in 1775. See *DAB*; I. C. C. Graham, *Colonists from Scotland* (Cornell University Press, 1956), 125–26.

**Buckingham House**
See *Tryon's Palace*

**Bull, William (1710–91), 21**
Son of a lieutenant-governor of South Carolina who died in 1755, Bull succeeded to the office in 1759 and was also acting governor for most of the time until he was stripped of power by the patriots in 1775. He stayed in the colony until British troops departed finally from Charleston in 1782, when he sailed with them to London and spent his last nine years of life there. See *DAB*.

**Buxton Spa, 84**

**Cameron, Alexander (d. 1781), 35**
A Scotsman, whose real name was possibly McLeod. Related to John Stuart by marriage and resident in Georgia by 1737. Became Stuart's deputy superintendent to the Cherokee in 1768 and lived much among them but in 1779 was made superintendent in the "western district," when Thomas Brown took the eastern district including the Cherokee. See Cashin, *The King's Ranger*.

**Cape Fear River,** 64–65

A large river of North Carolina, of several branches, whose estuary provided the colony's deepest and safest inlet for shipping, although not without shoals. The point of arrival of large numbers of Scottish emigrants in the early 1770s.

**Catawbas,** 23

**Ceded Lands,** 6, 35–38, 43, 47, 53–54, 59–60

See Records of the Commissioners for the Ceded Lands, at Surveyor General's Department of Georgia, Atlanta; Cashin, *Colonial Augusta*; Harper, *Travels of William Bartram*; De Vorsey, *Indian Boundary*, chap. 7; Alden, *John Stuart*, chap. 17; Robert S. Davis, ed., *The Wilkes County Papers, 1733–1833* (Easley, S.C., 1979); Alex M. Hitz, "The Earliest Settlers in Wilkes County," *Georgia Historical Quarterly*, 40, no. 3 (1956).

**Charlestown (now Charleston),** 6, 10, 12, 19–23, 26, 28–30, 32–33, 39–41, 45, 48–49, 51, 54–55, 58–59, 61, 63, 67, 91–92

Provincial capital of South Carolina and throughout the eighteenth century the main seaport and center of trade on the southern seaboard of British North America. Many merchants' houses of pre-1770 survive, including about ten in King Street where William Mylne lodged. These houses are generally detached, of two stories, built of brick and rendered, with three windows or two windows and a door facing the street, and their longer dimension perpendicular to the street. Facing the end of Broad Street is the imposing Exchange built in 1767–71 by John and Peter Horlbeck; its design is attributed to William Rigby Naylor. It is also of rendered brickwork but embellished with a three-bay portico and pediment, a central cupola and venetian windows with balustraded balconies to each side. It also served as Custom House and during the British occupation in 1780–82 had a prison in its cellar—hence its present name, the Old Exchange and Provost Dungeon. Cobbled pavings and some wharfside buildings remain along the original waterfront. The site of Charleston consisted of a marshy peninsula and the whole adjacent coastal plain was considered unhealthy for Europeans. See *This Is Charleston* (Charleston, S.C.: Carolina Art Association, 1976).

**Cherokees,** 6, 23, 34–35, 38, 56, 59

For general description, see De Vorsey, "The Colonial Georgia Backcountry," in Cashin, *Colonial Augusta*; De Vorsey, *The Indian Boundary*; Harper, *Travels of William Bartram*; Charles M. Hudson, "The Genesis of Georgia's Indians," in Jackson and Spalding, *Forty Years of Diversity*.

**Chesepeak Bay ferry (now Chesapeake),** 72

Had Mylne taken the ferry crossing of twenty-one miles from somewhere near Williamsburg, he would have gone by a route that traversed none of northern Virginia, nor the towns of Annapolis and Baltimore.

**Chickasaws,** 23, 34
See references under **Cherokees**

**Choctaws,** 23, 47, 56
See references under **Cherokees**

**Cleland's Yards**
See **Ferguson (Walter)**

**College of William and Mary,** 68
Chartered in 1693, with construction of its frontal building started in 1694, is the oldest college building surviving from British America. It is called the Wren Building because it was described in a book published in London in 1724 as "first modelled by Sir Christopher Wren, adapted to the nature of the country by the gentlemen there." It burned, except for the walls, in 1705, was rebuilt in 1710–16 but burned twice more in the nineteenth century. In 1928–31 it was restored following the design of 1716, with the help of a plan drawn by Thomas Jefferson in 1772 in connection with a proposed extension that was abandoned after only the foundations had been built. The rooms on the ground floor that Mylne mentions can be identified today, but he does less than justice to the building by omitting mention of the refectory (now the Great Hall) on the ground floor and the grand long gallery on the floor above. For references see **Williamsburgh (now Williamsburg)**.

**Congarees,** 55
A district near present-day Columbia, South Carolina; below the confluence of the Broad and Saluda rivers the river is called the Congaree.

**Cooley, Thomas,** 82–83

**Cooper River,** 61
River in South Carolina, lying on the eastern side of the Charleston peninsula.

**Creeks,** 6, 23–24, 34–35, 38, 46–47, 53, 56, 59
See references under **Cherokees**

**Curling, Captain Alexander,** 12, 14, 20–21
Master of the *London*, which carried on regular trade between London and Charleston.

**Delaware River,** 74
The tidal estuary extends from Delaware Bay past Philadelphia up to Trenton. There was no impediment to navigation until a bridge was built at Trenton in 1806.

**Drummond, George (1687–1766),** 3
Probably Edinburgh's greatest lord provost (i.e., leader of the town council), elected many times between 1725 and 1764. See M. Hook et al., *Lord*

*Provost George Drummond, 1687–1766* (Edinburgh: Scotland's Cultural Heritage, 1987).

**Dublin,** 82–83
Capital city of Ireland. Recognized in the second half of the eighteenth century as the second city of the British Empire, the seat of a strong and independent Irish parliament. Population was about 130,000 in 1750 rising to 200,000 by 1800. See John Harvey, *Dublin* (London: Batsford, 1949); J. T. Gilbert, ed., *Calendar of Ancient Records of Dublin*, vols. 12–14 (Dublin, 1889–1944).

**Dunmore, Lord (John Murray, 4th Earl of Dunmore [1732–1809]),** 72
Last royal governor of Virginia. He sat as a representative Scottish Peer in the House of Lords in 1761–70 and 1776–84 and was appointed governor of New York in 1770 and transferred to Virginia in 1771. In 1773 he went to the northwest frontier of the province and built Fort Dunmore, on the site of modern Pittsburgh, for defense against the Indians. After a force of white militia had defeated the Shawnee in 1774, Dunmore made a treaty with the Indians. He was a respected and popular governor until he twice dissolved the provincial Assembly because it supported American rejections of control by the British Parliament. In June 1775 he went on board a warship for safety and attempted from there to govern the colony and subdue it by force; but a year later he disbanded his troops and left for England. From 1787 to 1796 he was again in the colonies as governor of the Bahamas. See *DNB*; *DAB*; Cashin, *The King's Ranger*.

**East India Company,** 6–7, 10–11, 20–21
The company was chartered by Queen Elizabeth I in 1600. See *The Annual Register*, 1773; Griswold, *The Boston Tea Party*.

**Edinburgh,** 1, 3, 5, 7–10, 39–40, 54, 57–59, 61–62, 78–83, 91–92
Capital of Scotland, which had lost its national parliament in 1707 and was subject to the parliament of the united kingdom of England, Scotland, and Wales sitting in London. The courts, established church, and some other elements of government remained separate. See A. J. Youngson, *The Making of Classical Edinburgh* (Edinburgh University Press, 1966); Ruddock, "North Bridge, Edinburgh."

**Elliock, James Veitch, Lord,** 8–9, 39, 45, 78–80, 82
Judge of the highest Scottish court, the Court of Session.

**Emistisiguo,** 38, 47
Creek headman of exceptional character and influence, on whom John Stuart, David Taitt, and Thomas Brown relied greatly in their dealings with the Creek Nation. See Alden, *John Stuart*; Cashin, *The King's Ranger*.

## ANNOTATED INDEX

**The Exchange (Charleston),** 20–21
See **Charlestown (now Charleston)**

**The Exchange (London),** 14
The center of commerce in London. An imposing building ranged round an open court and lying between Cornhill and Threadneedle Street. Built in 1667–71 to the design of Edward Jerman, it had undergone major repairs after a fire in 1747 and some improvements by George Dance, clerk of the city works, in 1767–68. It was finally destroyed by fire in 1838. See Colvin, *Biographical Dictionary*, 460; Maitland, *History of London*, vol. 2, 898–903.

**Ferguson (Walter),** 52
Writer to the Signet (i.e., solicitor and attorney) in Edinburgh. He proposed building on land that he had "feued" adjoining the site of the intended Register House for Scotland at the east end of the New Town and north end of the new Edinburgh North Bridge. His intention was contested by the feu superior, backed by the town council, who held control of development in all other parts of the New Town. The Court of Session ruled against the superior on July 30, 1773, and the House of Lords in London rejected an appeal on March 3, 1774, giving victory to Ferguson.

**Florida,** 31

**Fort Augusta,** 23
See "Fort Augusta," *Georgia Magazine* (Aug.–Sept. 1966); T. Heard and Thomas H. Robertson, "The Town and Fort of Augusta"; and Larry E. Ivers, "The Soldiers of Fort Augusta," in Cashin, *Colonial Augusta*.

**Fort Charlotte,** 43
Stone fort built in 1767 by Andrew Williamson with £1,000 from the South Carolina Assembly for frontier protection when Fort Moore was abandoned. It was one mile below the confluence of the Broad with the Savannah River and adjacent to a ford. See Alden, *John Stuart*, 189n.

**Fort James,** 37, 42–43
See "Fort James," *Georgia Magazine* (Feb.–Mar. 1968): 19–21.

**Fort Moore,** 22
A fort built in 1716 on the South Carolina side of the Savannah River about three miles downstream from the site of Augusta for protection of the Indian trade. Abandoned in favor of Fort Charlotte in 1765. See Alden, *John Stuart*, 189n.

**Fort Natchez,** 53
A British outpost on the east bank of the Mississippi over two hundred miles from the mouth. Taken by a Spanish force sent from New Orleans in 1778.

**The "Forty-Five,"** 5
Popular name for the Jacobite rising that took place in 1745, when the

"Young Pretender," Prince Charles Edward Stuart, returned to Scotland and "raised the clans" against the Hanover monarchy. After initial successes he led his army south as far as the middle of England, but was then persuaded to withdraw to Scotland and suffered heavy defeat at Culloden, near Inverness, in April 1746. After five months in hiding he escaped to France, from which he had hoped for decisive military support which never arrived. It was the last of the militant Jacobite risings in Great Britain. See A. J. Youngson, *The Prince and the Pretender* (London, Croom Helm, 1985).

**George III (1738–1820), 6–7**
King of the united kingdom of England, Scotland, and Wales, 1760–1820. The first of the Hanoverian kings to be truly British.

**Georgetown, 61, 63**
Important seaport in South Carolina with an extensive hinterland of rich plantations in the 1770s, exporting rice, indigo, and timber. It was planned in 1735–37 as a grid of five streets parallel to the waterfront with nine crossing them at right angles. Merchants owning property on the landward side of Bay Street (now renamed Front Street) were permitted to build wharves and stores on the waterfront side. These merchants' houses may be those to which William Mylne attributed fine prospects. The town lies on Winyah Bay, a long tidal inlet into which the Sampit, Black, Great, and Little Peedee rivers all discharge. See G. C. Rogers, *History of Georgetown County, SC*.

**Georgia,** 6, 19, 22–25, 28, 34–38, 46–47, 53–56, 58, 65

**Georgia Gazette,** 46, 59

**Gibb, Dr. (Robert),** 63
Son of Francis Gibb, a writer (i.e., solicitor and attorney) in Edinburgh. Studied medicine at Edinburgh University. Emigrated in 1754 to Georgetown, South Carolina, where he practiced medicine. Later he bought large plantations on which he had fifty-six slaves. Died at Georgetown 1777 when facing banishment for refusing an oath of abjuration of the Crown. His estate was confiscated and sold by the State of South Carolina in 1782. He died a bachelor and his only sister filed a loyalist claim in London for £4,300 for loss of his estate. She was awarded £3,000. See G. C. Rogers, *History of Georgetown County, SC*, 93; AO 13/132 at PRO.

**Gordon, James,** 36–37, 41–48, 50, 53, 59–60
Native of Orkney and evidently respected as a gentleman. He went into partnership with Jonas and Thomas Brown to purchase a tract of the Ceded Lands and settle it with British emigrants. Though he failed to raise his share of the capital he traveled to Georgia some months ahead of Thomas Brown, having borrowed £30 from Jonas to pay his fare. On behalf of the partnership he was issued, presumably in his absence, with warrants for a survey of 1,000 acres on the Broad River and 4,000 on its tributary Chickasaw Creek on Novem-

ber 16, 1773. On his own account he either bought (as he inferred later) or rented the plantation of New Richmond, of more than three hundred acres on the Carolina side of the Savannah about two miles above Augusta, and on which LeRoy Hammond had built a very expensive house in 1771. He signed the Loyalist resolution in St. Paul's Parish, which was published in the *Georgia Gazette* on October 12, 1774. After Brown left Augusta in August 1775, Gordon remained, met their second ship-load of immigrants at Savannah in December, led them to Brownsborough and maintained them with food and clothing for twelve months, but he failed to prevent their complete dispersal during the next few years. He returned to working his plantation on the Carolina side with some slaves, escaping persecution as a Loyalist through "the favour and protection of the rebel general Williamson," but some time after Brown had retaken Augusta for the Crown in 1780 he was forced by the rebels to flee his plantation by canoe with only three trunks of personal effects. These he left with Brown at the new fort, which fell in 1781. In 1786 in Nova Scotia Gordon filed a loyalist claim on the British government, including among the property he had lost two stills valued at £150, which he had intended to operate in partnership with Andrew Robertson. Most of his claim was struck out as referring to property for which the Browns had provided all the funds, but Gordon himself received £117. He had taken a wife from among his slaves and with her settled in the Bahamas in 1787. Their attachment was such that after her death he refused to bury her body and kept it, dressed and bejewelled, in a protective cage. See Records of the Commissioners for the Ceded Lands, at the Surveyor-General's Department of Georgia, Atlanta; AO 12 and 13 at PRO; Cashin, *The King's Ranger*.

**Gordon, Sir John, Baronet** (ca. 1725–95), 79–81, 88
Baronet, of Earlstone in Galloway. Married Anne Mylne in 1775. As he died childless his title passed to a nephew, also John, whose father had established a plantation in Jamaica before 1775 and called it Earlstone after the family home. The family seat, Earlstone Castle in Kirkcudbrightshire, was a tower house of early fortified type, acquired by the Gordons by marriage in 1615. See Mylne Papers, GD1/51, at SRO; D. McGibbon and T. Ross, *Castellated and Domestic Architecture of Scotland*, vol. 3 (1889), 521–23.

**Gordon, Lady,**
See **Mylne, Anne**

**Governor's palace,** 71
Located in Williamsburg, Va., was built between 1706 and 1720 under the supervision of, and possibly designed by, Henry Cary, a builder and architect. The interior was remodelled in the 1750s, but the whole palace was destroyed by fire in 1781. It was rebuilt on the original foundations in the 1930s. The "additions . . . made from time to time" that Mylne mentions must include some of the work around 1750 and the ballroom wing completed in 1754. For references, see **Williamsburgh (now Williamsburg)**.

**Halkerstone's Wynd,** 8, 10

One of the many wynds, too narrow to be called streets, that stretched from the High Street of old Edinburgh down the hillside to the flat ground near the Nor' Loch. In 1715 William Mylne's grandfather built a "land," or tenement, of dwellings there. Most of the property passed to his children and grandchildren, but much of it was destroyed by fire in 1756. William lived there from his return to Edinburgh in 1758 until his departure in 1773. The south approach to the new bridge that he built in 1765–73 was immediately adjacent and parallel, and must have cast deep shadow over the wynd and at least the lower parts of the building. See Robert Mylne, family history at BAL; *Plan of the City and Castle of Edinburgh by Willm. Edgar,* 1765.

**Hallifax (correctly Halifax),** 67

Town on the Roanoke River that became the first seat of revolutionary government in North Carolina. See H. T. Lefler and W. S. Powell, *Colonial North Carolina* (New York, 1973).

**Hatfield (or Hatefield), John,** 19–20, 28, 33, 40–41, 45, 56, 58

Merchant in Charleston, at least from 1765 when he married Sarah Swallow there. Sarah was probably the daughter of Mrs. Swallow, a tavern keeper. Hatfield received land grants of 950 acres, mostly in Craven County, in 1764–75. He and his family remained in America after the Revolution. He was apparently known to William Mylne and intended to be his postal address before William left London. In 1773–75 he lived or traded in King Street. A twentieth-century historian has stated that King Street "was then chiefly the resort of hucksters, peddlers and tavern keepers." See land grant books at South Carolina Archives, Columbia; L. Sellers, *Charleston Business on the Eve of the American Revolution* (New York, 1970), 81.

**Hawks, John** (1731–90), 65

English architect taken to North Carolina by William Tryon in 1764, having been at some time previously "in the service of Mr Leadbeater," presumed to be Stiff Leadbetter, a London architect who on his death in 1766 was succeeded in the office of surveyor to St. Paul's Cathedral by Robert Mylne. Hawks designed the capitol/governor's house for Tryon at his newly chosen provincial capital, New Bern, and also contracted in 1767 to oversee the building of it. He has been called "America's first professional architect," but he was also an able accountant and held a number of public offices before, during, and after the Revolution. See *DAB*; F. Kimball and G. S. Carraway, "Tryon's Palace," *New York Historical Society Quarterly Bulletin* 24 (1940): 13–22; A. T. Dill, "Eighteenth-Century New Bern: Part VI," *North Carolina Historical Review* 23 (1946): 142–71; Colvin, *Biographical Dictionary*, 508.

**Hearts of Steel,** 75

A large body of Presbyterian tenants in Ulster, Ireland, who protested in 1771–73 against the imposition of huge rent increases as their leases became due for renewal and consequently lost their holdings to newcomers. Adopting the name "Hearts of Steel" they roamed the countty maiming the cattle and wrecking the property of the newcomers. By intimidating witnesses or juries, they at first obtained the release of those of their number who were arrested and tried. When the tide turned and some members were executed, thousands left Ireland for America and the movement collapsed; but in the colonies they soon formed a significant and strongly anti-British component of the Continental army. See W. E. H. Lecky, *History of England in the Eighteenth Century*, vol. 4 (1882), 348–55.

### Hogg and Kinlochs, 57, 59, 76
Otherwise Kinloch and Hogg, or Kinlochs. Evidently bankers and represented in the Edinburgh directories by Thomas Hogg, banker in Kinlochs Close. Of Kinlochs who might have been Hogg's partner(s) the most likely are David Kinloch of Gilmerton, Esq., with an address in the Exchange, and Robert Kinloch of Kinmonth, Esq., of Blackfriars Wynd. See *Williamson's Directories*.

### Huntington, Lady (Selina Hastings, countess of Huntingdon {1707–91}), 17
Widow of the ninth earl of Huntingdon (d. 1746), she was a friend of Whitefield, the Wesleys, and other evangelical leaders, supported many chaplains and itinerant preachers, financed the building of chapels in several towns, the establishment of a seminary in North Wales, and mission work in America. She was particularly keen to reach the upper classes with her evangelical message. See *DNB*.

### Islay, 5
Large island off the west coast of Scotland.

### Islington, 16, 85
A suburb about two miles north of the center of the City of London. The New River, which was a channel supplied from the springs of Chadwell and Amwell twenty miles north of London and first cut in 1609–13, flowed south through Islington to a circular storage pond near the crossroads now known as the Angel, providing piped water for most of the city. Houses were built by the New River Company near the river at Islington in 1768, and Robert Mylne had his office and residence as engineer to the company there. See Samuel Smiles, *Lives of the Engineers* (1904 ed.), I, 58–99; Richardson, *Robert Mylne*.

### James River, 68, 72
A major river of Virginia with an estuary several miles wide over a length of at least sixty miles. William Mylne probably crossed it by ferry to Jamestown, the port for Williamsburg standing four miles from it on the north shore of the estuary.

**Ker,** 28
Possibly George Kerr, tinplate worker, of Netherbow, Edinburgh.

**Kinlochs**
See **Hogg and Kinlochs.**

**Learmont, Jock,** 15
Probably John Learmonth, tanner, of Saint Mary's Wynd, Edinburgh, or William Learmonth, vintner, of Halkerston's Wynd, or a relative of either. The nickname "Jock" is applied to Scotsmen of any name.

**Leger and Greenwood,** 20

**Leith,** 10, 14, 39, 50
Seaport for Edinburgh. Only two miles from the Old Town of Edinburgh, on the shore of the Firth of Forth, it had the largest trade on the east coast of Scotland in the eighteenth century. See H. Arnot, *The History of Edinburgh* (Edinburgh, 1779), 570–603.

**Little River,** 23–25, 35, 38, 43
Tributary of the Savannah River on the Georgia side; its confluence with the river is some twenty miles above Augusta. In 1763–73 it was the northern limit of white settlement.

**Livingston, Charles,** 17, 29, 33, 45, 49, 51–53, 76, 78–80, 89
Writer (i.e., solicitor and attorney) in Edinburgh who had been William Mylne's legal agent for some years prior to 1773. See Mylne Papers, GD1/51 at SRO; *Williamson's Directories*.

**London,** 3, 6–7, 10–11, 14–16, 21–22, 24, 27–28, 34–36, 39, 47, 49, 51, 58, 78, 80, 83, 91–92
Capital of the United Kingdom on the north bank of the River Thames, a city of some seven hundred thousand inhabitants, including the suburbs, in the 1770s. Considerable development had been taking place outside the walls, starting with the royal residence and center of national government at Westminster, just over a mile to the west, and spreading north, east, and south on the other side of the river. These and later expansions have remained outside the boundary of the City of London, an area of only one square mile. See Weinreb and Hibbert, *London Encyclopaedia*.

**McDonald, Flora** (1722–90), 65
Heroine of Prince Charles Edward Stuart's escape from the royal army in the western isles of Scotland in 1746, after the failure of the last attempt to restore the Stuarts to the throne of Great Britain by force of arms. Rising rents and several bad seasons in the islands forced her emigration in the summer of 1774 with her husband Allan McDonald (see **Barrisdale**), two of their sons, and eight indentured servants. They spent some time with relations at Mount Pleasant, North Carolina (now Cameron's Hill), before Allan bought

525 acres of land, already partly cleared, in Anson County. Almost immediately, in June 1775, Allan took the lead in forming a local loyalist militia, largely of Scottish highlanders. He was one of their officers in the disastrous Battle of Moore's Creek-Bridge in February 1776, and was captured and imprisoned for eighteen months. Flora stayed on the land until she lost it by confiscation in 1777. She obtained a safe conduct to rejoin Allan, now free in New York. In failing health she accompanied him to Nova Scotia to rejoin a British regiment, but she left for London in 1779 and got back to the Isle of Skye in July 1780. Allan remained in Nova Scotia until his regiment was disbanded in 1783, when he received a grant of land, but went to London to present a loyalist claim for compensation for his losses in North Carolina. In response to a claim for £1,341 he received only £440, and went to Skye to join Flora. They survived in the islands without a fixed home until Flora's death in 1790. Allan moved back into his old home at Kingsburgh, now tenanted by his daughter's father-in-law, and died there two years later. See *DNB*; A. R. MacDonald, *The Truth About Flora MacDonald* (Edinburgh, 1938); E. G. Vining, *Flora* (Philadelphia, Lippincott), 1966.

### Mackay, Francis, 57

Probably Francis Mackay of Browen (also spelled *Bruan*) in Latheron Parish, Caithness, who married Catherine Calder at Wick on October 20, 1733. Presumably a kinsman of Robert Mackay. See Wick Parish Register, 1701–56, at SRO.

### Mackay, Mrs. (Mary, née Malbone [d. 1797]), 50, 60

Widow of a Mr. Chilcott. She accompanied her daughter Catherine to Augusta when Catherine married John Francis Williams around 1769. Mary married Robert Mackay, probably in 1771. She lived in Augusta with their son Robert Mackay II ("Bob") during the Revolution and was in poor circumstances until he became a merchant. See Mackay-Stiles Papers, University of North Carolina Library, no. 470, vol. 42; Robert Mackay Papers, Colonial Dames of America Collection, Georgia Historical Society; W. C. Hartridge, *The Letters of Robert Mackay {II} to His Wife* (Athens, Ga., 1949); M. F. Norwood, "History of the White House Tract"; H. Callahan, "Colonial Life in Augusta," in Cashin, *Colonial Augusta*, 96–119.

### Mackay, Robert (d. 1775), 28–30, 41, 46–47, 50, 55–60, 76, 80

Merchant in Augusta. Probably born in Caithness, northern Scotland, ca. 1730, but the detailed published records of the Church of Scotland and the Scottish Episcopal Church do not support the belief of Robert II in later years that his paternal grandfather was "the minister or clergyman of Wick." Robert Mackay emigrated, according to his son's story, to Kingston, Jamaica, as a young man, later lived at Havana, Cuba, and Charleston and Beaufort, South Carolina, before reaching Augusta. He was established there by 1767 as one of the leading merchants who supplied and bought from the men who traded with the Indians. At some time he formed a partnership with John Francis Williams but dissolved it in 1770. He was owner of the five-hundred-acre "White House Tract" on the northern fringe of Augusta, with a large white house of stone that had long been used as a trading post (see **Brown, Thomas**). He married Mary Malbone Chilcott about 1771 and Robert II was born in 1772. He signed the Loyalist resolution in Saint Paul's Parish that was published on October 12, 1774. Died at Augusta on October 30, 1775. For references, see **Mackay, Mary**. Also see Cashin, *The King's Ranger*; *Fasti Ecclesiae Scoticanae*, vol. 7 (1928), 77–143; J. B. Craven, *History of the Episcopal Church in the Diocese of Caithness* (Kirkwall, Orkney, 1908).

**Mackay, Robert II ("Bob"), (1772–1816), 60**
Son of Robert and Mary Mackay, born June 23, 1772, at Augusta. Lived there with his mother during the Revolution, was then educated in Edinburgh for six years; later became a prosperous merchant, as well as port warden and justice of the peace, in Savannah. For references, see **Mackay, Mary**.

**McLean, Andrew, 46**

**Mad Turkey, 38**

**Mansfields, 18, 76**
Bankers in the Luckenbooths, Edinburgh. Listed as "Mansfield Hunter and Co." in 1774–75 and "Mansfield Ramsay and Co." in 1775–78. See *Williamson's Directories*.

**Maryland, 55, 72–73, 75**

**Millar, Mr., 77**
Probably Patrick Millar, banker, of James's Court, Edinburgh, or one of several Millars, merchants, of the Luckenbooths in High Street, Edinburgh.

**Minories, 16**
Street in London occupied in 1720 chiefly by gunsmiths but taken over by mixed trading in the nineteenth century. The street was "improved" to the plans of George Dance, Jr., about 1768. See Weinreb and Hibbert, *London Encyclopaedia*.

**Mobile, 53**
A seaboard settlement in West Florida, near the head of the estuary of the Alabama River. Founded by Bienville, governor of French Louisiana, in 1710, it was garrisoned by the British when West Florida was ceded to them in 1763. It fell to a Spanish force from New Orleans in 1779.

**Mobility, 75**
Used to mean "mob," occasionally before and commonly during the American Revolution; usually civilians gathered for a show of strength.

ANNOTATED INDEX 113

**Moorfields, 15**
The moor outside the wall of London was drained in 1527, but a considerable area of open space remained in the eighteenth century, with Bedlam (Bethlehem Hospital) built along its southern margin just outside the city wall. See Maitland, *History of London*.

**Mother.** See **Mylne, Elizabeth (née Duncan)**

**Mumford, Colonel, 67**
Possibly Robert *Munford* (d. 1784), a Virginian aristocrat who served in the French-Indian wars in 1758. He was lieutenant of Mecklenburg County, Virginia, and representative in the legislature from 1765, and courageous on the side of liberty before and during the Revolution; but notable also as a lover of literature and author of plays, verse, and a translation of Ovid. See *DAB*.

**Mungo, 14–16, 50, 55, 60–61, 63**
William Mylne's dog, who accompanied him from Edinburgh.

**Murray, 65**
A member of the family Murray, which held large property at Philiphaugh, by Selkirk in southern Scotland. Filed a loyalist claim in London that included 110 acres, a "capital mansion," ten negroes, bonds, and interest due, all in Georgia and valued together at £4,387, as well as large land holdings in North Carolina. He left Georgia for Britain in 1776 but returned in 1778 and immediately joined the Royal Army, as a result of which his property was confiscated in 1782 and he and his family returned to Great Britain. See AO 13/36 at PRO.

**Mylne, Anne (1745–1822), 3, 12–18, 25–30, 33, 39–45, 47–59, 61–77, 78–79, 80–84, 88, 91–92**
William's sister. Married Sir John Gordon in 1775, becoming Lady Gordon. See Mylne Papers, GD1/51, at SRO, which contain many letters and other documents.

**Mylne, Elizabeth (née Duncan) (d. 1778), 10, 17, 29, 33, 40, 45, 52, 58, 77, 79–81, 84, 91**
Mother of Robert, William, Elizabeth (Selby), and Anne.

**Mylne, Robert (1633–1710), 1**
Master mason to King Charles II and Queen Anne. A very successful and accomplished mason/architect. See R. S. Mylne, *Master Masons*; Colvin, *Biographical Dictionary*, 570–71; Robert Mylne, family history, BAL.

**Mylne, Robert (1733–1811), 1, 3, 8–9, 12–13, 16–18, 27, 29–34, 39, 45, 49, 51–52, 76, 78, 80–83, 85–88, 91–92**
William's elder brother. See R. S. Mylne, *Master Masons*; Colvin, *Biographical Dictionary*, 571–77; C. Gotch, "The Missing Years of Robert Mylne," *Archi-*

*tectural Review* (Sept. 1951): 179–82; Richardson, *Robert Mylne*; Ruddock, *Arch Bridges*.

**Mylne, William (1734–90)**
See R. S. Mylne, *Master Masons*; Colvin, *Biographical Dictionary*, 578; C. Gotch, "The Missing Years of Robert Mylne"; Ruddock, *Arch Bridges*; Ruddock, "North Bridge, Edinburgh"; J. T. Gilbert, ed., *Calendar of Ancient Records of Dublin*, vols. 12–14 (Dublin, 1889–1944); Mylne Papers, GD1/51 at SRO; Mylne Papers at BAL; Betham abstracts of prerogatory wills, vol. 49, fol. 141, at Public Record Office, Dublin.

**Mylne, William Chadwell (1781–1863),** 82, 88
Only surviving son of Robert Mylne (1733–1811). Civil engineer and occasional architect. Succeeded his father as engineer to the New River Company, 1811–61. See Colvin, *Biographical Dictionary*, 578; R. S. Mylne, *Master Masons*.

**Netherclift, Thomas (d. 1793),** 57
Merchant in Savannah at least from 1766 to 1793. He obtained many grants of land in coastal parishes in 1769–75 and represented Saint Paul's Parish in the provincial assembly in 1774. Friend and associate in business of Robert Mackay. See *Georgia Gazette*; Norwood, *History of the White House Tract*; Robert Mackay Papers, in Colonial Dames of America Collection, Georgia Historical Society.

**Neuse River,** 67
River in North Carolina, joined by the Trent River at New Bern, then opening into an estuary that discharges into the huge shallows of Pamlico Sound. Seagoing vessels had to pass the narrow Ocracoke Inlet from the sound to the Atlantic. See C. C. Crittenden, "Ships and Shipping in North Carolina, 1763–1789," *North Carolina Historical Review*, 8 (1931): 1–13.

**Newburn (correctly New Bern),** 65–67
Capital of North Carolina from 1765, when William Tryon became governor, until the end of the Revolution. Its potential for external trade was limited by the navigational difficulties (see **Neuse River**) and in 1775 it was still a small town.

**New Orleans,** 53
Founded and built as capital of the French province of Louisiana in 1718–22; both town and province were in Spanish hands in the 1770s.

**New Richmond,** 37, 40, 43, 47, 54, 59, 91–92
A plantation of 300–450 acres on the South Carolina side of the Savannah River about five miles upstream from Augusta. (William's estimate of three miles is inaccurate.) Occupied by James Gordon at least from mid-1774 (but said in his loyalist claim to have been paid for only in 1775 at £300, not including the house) it was also the location of Thomas Brown's clash with

ANNOTATED INDEX 115

the Sons of Liberty on August 1, 1775. See AO 12 and 13 at PRO London; W. Brown, *The King's Friends* (Providence, 1965); Robert Mills, *Atlas of South Carolina* (1825); Cashin, *The King's Ranger*.

**New River Company,** 83, 88
See also Islington.

**New Windsor,** 22–23

**New York,** 10, 12, 20, 48, 55, 58, 61–62, 67, 77, 92
First settled by the Dutch in 1614 as New Amsterdam, taken over by the British in 1664 as New York. In the early 1770s a rapidly expanding city of about twenty thousand inhabitants, the center of trade and finance for the middle colonies and of growing educational and social importance. Well connected by ferries and packets to other islands and the mainland. It filled the space between both shores of the southern end of Manhattan Island, with a consequent irregular street plan much of which still exists. The domestic, commercial, and public buildings were of stone and brick, both the buildings and population betraying a considerable but declining Dutch influence. Rebel activity and fire caused considerable destruction in 1775–76. See B. Ratzer, *Map of New York City* (1767); J. Morse, *American Geography* (1792); W. P. Cumming, *British Maps of Colonial America* (Chicago, 1974), 83.

**Nicoll, John,** 79
Clearly a creditor of William Mylne, but of various Nicols and Nichols listed as trading in Edinburgh in 1773–78 none is named John and only one, David Nicol, a smith, seems a likely creditor.

**Norfolk,** 72
Virginian seaport on the southern shore of the entry to Chesapeake Bay; a port of growing trade in the 1770s.

**North, Lord (Frederick North, second Earl of Guildford [1732–92]),** 6, 7
Prime minister of the Tory government in London under King George III from 1770 to 1782.

**North Bridge, Edinburgh,** 5, 7–9, 76
High masonry bridge of five arches built 1765–75 to connect the old town of Edinburgh with the newly planned "New Town" to the north. See Ruddock, "North Bridge, Edinburgh."

**North Carolina,** 6, 19, 26, 36, 38, 55, 67–68, 75

**Oconee River,** 43, 47
Major river in upper Georgia west of the Ogeechee and running south-southeast to a confluence with the Ocmulgee to form the Altamaha River.

**Ogeechee River,** 24, 38, 43, 47
River in Georgia west of and roughly parallel to the Savannah. In upper Georgia it was the western limit of permitted white settlement by the proclamations of 1763 and 1773.

**Ogilvey (correctly Mr. Charles Ogilvie),** 57–59
A merchant who after living for some years in Charleston had gone home to run his business from Britain; visited South Carolina in 1773, leaving Charleston again for London in August 1774. When he went to South Carolina again in 1780 he sided with the restored colonial government, which resulted in confiscation of his very extensive estate in 1782. Large loyalist claims were made by his heirs. See AO 12 and 13 at PRO.

**Oglethorpe, General James Edward (1696–1785),** 22
English soldier and philanthropist who, though educated at Eton and Oxford, had strong Jacobite sympathies in early life; became the leading trustee of the new colony of Georgia, accompanying the first party of settlers who landed at the site of Savannah in 1733 and living in the colony for most of its early years. See *DNB*; *DAB*; Milton L. Ready, "Philanthropy and the Origins of Georgia," and P. Spalding, "James Edward Oglethorpe's Quest for an American Zion," in Jackson and Spalding, *Forty Years of Diversity.*

**Orkney,** 36–37, 50, 53
A group of islands off the north coast of Scotland and a port of call for emigrant ships that set out from ports on the east coast of Britain.

**Ottaway River,** 68
Now called Nottaway River. A fairly small river in Virginia flowing southward to enter the Albemarle Sound in North Carolina.

**Penn, William (1644–1718),** 74
Quaker founder of the colony of Pennsylvania.

**Pennsylvania,** 26, 55, 72–73, 75

**Pensacola,** 53
The largest white settlement in West Florida, which was a British territory after 1763. John Stuart, the superintendent of Indian affairs, was there organizing supplies of arms for Britain's Indian allies in 1776–77. After his death in 1779 it held out against the Spaniards until 1781.

**Philadelphia,** 10, 12, 19–20, 46, 48, 73–74
Founded by William Penn as capital city of his newly chartered territory of Pennsylvania in 1682 and laid out to his order with a chessboard pattern of streets to reach from the Delaware River to the Schuylkill. By 1770 it was the largest city in any of the colonies, with at least thirty thousand inhabitants. It was the meeting-place of the first Continental Congress in September 1774 and of the second Congress in May 1775. It was a well-appointed city with a

city hall, the Colony House, a college and Pennsylvania Hospital, all built in the 1740s or 1750s, and the new Stone Prison, of 1774. The main street running from river to river, called Market or High Street, was one hundred feet wide, allowing the market to occupy the middle of the street. The market had been rebuilt and enlarged in 1773 to a total length of 1300 feet, stretching three whole blocks from Front street to Fourth. It consisted of a wide middle aisle under a continuous ceiling for the buying public; wide brick piers at each side supporting the roof and ceiling and also providing part-enclosed spaces, under the overhang of the roof, for the sellers' stalls. See W. Birch and Son, *The City of Philadelphia as It Appeared in 1800*, 28 plates (Philadelphia, 1800).

**Potowmack River (now Potomac),** 72
A large river on the boundary between Virginia and Maryland.

**Pouderhall (or Powderhall),** 10-11, 15, 32, 39, 56, 59, 80–81
A house about one and a half miles northeast of old Edinburgh, on or close to the old Bonnington road and on the south side of the Water of Leith, which is called in one of William Mylne's letters "Powderhall Water." Described in 1883 as a "quaint little mansion-house . . . down in a dell," it was bought or built by Thomas Mylne, William's father. William's mother lived there until her death, as did Anne until her marriage in 1775. In 1774, and probably for several years after, "little Will" was also there in the care of Anne and later of her mother. After the latter's death in 1778 Robert and Elizabeth Selby moved into Powderhall. When Elizabeth died it was advertised for sale in 1798 and sold for £2,000 in 1800. It was demolished in the twentieth century. See Mylne Papers, GD1/51, at SRO; letters of Robert Mylne, in Mylne Papers at BAL; J. Grant, *Old and New Edinburgh*, vol. 3 (Edinburgh, 1883), 88–93.

**Queensborough,** 46
A township beside the Ogeechee River settled in the late 1760s by a large group of "Scotch-Irish" families (i.e., Presbyterians from the northern counties of Ireland). By 1771 about 270 Irish families were there. See De Vorsey, *The Indian Boundary*; De Vorsey, *De Brahm's Report of the General Survey in the Southern District of North America* (Columbia: University of South Carolina Press, 1971).

**Ramsay,** 28
Robert Ramsay, tailor, of Gray's Close, Edinburgh.

**Rappahanock River,** 72

**Roanoke River,** 67
A large river in North Carolina. At the time of Mylne's travels it was lined with plantations and used for inland navigation.

**Robertson (or Robinson), Andrew,** 35–36, 41–46, 56
Kinsman of the Mylnes, but the relationship has not been determined. Settled in South Carolina in 1756 and moved to Georgia in 1773. For service to the governor in "settling accounts" between Indians and their white creditors, he received free grants in the Ceded Lands. He signed a Loyalist protest in Savannah in August 1774; in 1777 he took an oath to fulfil his duties as a magistrate under the rebel government, but no oath of allegiance. He had bought a plantation on the Carolina side of the Savannah River about eight miles below its confluence with the Broad River, and he lived there from 1775 to 1780, when he moved at the order of Lieutenant Colonel Thomas Brown into Augusta and there lost all his slaves and movable property when the revolutionary forces recaptured the town. He reached London with his wife and seven children in 1782, with his Georgia lands confiscated and his Carolina property abandoned. In response to his Loyalist claim he received an immediate pension of £100 per annum and much later a lump sum of £1,220. See AO 12 and 13 at PRO; Records of Commissioners for the Ceded Lands, State of Georgia Archives; South Carolina Royal Grant Book 36, pp. 39–42, State of South Carolina Archives.

**Robinson, Duncan,** 28
Probably Duncan Robertson, merchant, of Saint Bernard's Street, Leith.

**Saint Augustine,** 31
Capital city of East Florida and a vital seaport for trade and war in the eighteenth century.

**Saint Pauls,** 15
Saint Paul's Cathedral in the City of London. Designed by Sir Christopher Wren and built in 1675–1710.

**Saint Paul's Parish,** 23, 46
The parish surrounding Augusta, created in 1758.

**Saint Pierre, Louis de,** 42–43
Frenchman trying in 1773–74 to establish wine-making at New Bordeaux (site of present Bordeaux in McCormick County, S.C.), close to Savannah River on the Carolina side some miles downstream from the confluence with the Broad River. When visited by William Bartram in June 1776 he had "a very thriving vineyard consisting of about five acres" as well as "very extensive . . . plantations of Indian corn (zea), rice, wheat, oats, indigo, convolvulus batata, etc." He wrote a book on grape and wine production in the colonies, which was published in London in 1772. See Harper, *Travels of Wm. Bartram,* 237, 393; *South Carolina Gazette,* Oct. 18 and Nov. 22, 1773.

**Savannah,** 22, 26, 32, 37–38, 41, 44, 46–47, 50–51, 53–54, 56–57, 59–60
First settlement and capital of Georgia. It has a good natural harbor that was

developed after 1750 in the tidal estuary of the Savannah River. The charming street plan, with open tree-planted squares placed on the intersections of streets, rather than occupying blocks between the streets, was laid down when the settlers first arrived. See Peter Gordon, *View of Savannah* (1734).

Savannah River, 22, 24–25, 31, 35, 37, 40, 42–43
A large river that forms the boundary between Georgia and South Carolina. In the eighteenth century it was navigated by boats of at least twenty tons burden from Savannah to Augusta, with some merchants running regular services. There was some carriage of crops from further inland in canoes. See Cashin, *Colonial Augusta*; Harper, *Travels of Wm. Bartram*, 200.

Schuyl Kill River (correctly Schuylkill), 74
River forming the western boundary of the original plan of Philadelphia.

Selby, Elizabeth (née Mylne) (d. 1797?), 33, 52, 81
Sister of Robert, William, and Anne. Eloped and married Robert Selby in the autumn of 1758 against her parents' wishes. Continued his plumbing business based at Powderhall after his death. See Mylne Papers at BAL; Mylne Papers, GD1/51 at SRO.

Selby, Robert (d. 1788), 40, 52, 54, 61–62, 76, 82
Plumber in Bailie Fyfe's Close, Edinburgh, 1773–84, replaced by James Selby in 1786–88. Married Elizabeth Mylne in 1758. They had three daughters, who were sent to a boarding school in Yorkshire. Two of them survived him and were executors of his will. William Mylne thought Selby "had good hands," and he was apparently successful as a plumber, but less so in "wild projects" that he embarked on. "Twice," William wrote in 1789, "did I save him from ruin, when he took to his bed in vexation at his folly, and all from a desire of money." See Mylne Papers at BAL; Mylne Papers, GD1/51 at SRO; *Williamson's Directories*.

Selbys (family), 16–17, 29, 40, 52, 58, 76, 79

Shawanese (correctly Shawnees), 56
Tribe located mainly in western Virginia.

Skye, 5
Large island off the west coast of Scotland, from which substantial numbers emigrated to the colonies in the early 1770s.

Smith, Roger, 20

Sons of Liberty, 6, 54
The name applied to bands of radicals who convened in many colonial ports and towns at various times from the Stamp Act protests of 1765 to the end of the Revolution. They commonly used strong-arm methods both in recruiting support for their own views and in demonstrating to the British and the Loy-

alists that tampering with colonists' freedom was going to produce violent reactions.

**South Amboy, 75**
A coastal town of New Jersey from which one could travel by packet boat directly to New York or, alternatively, go by road to Elizabethtown and take a shorter ferry—but still twenty-eight miles—to New York. William Mylne's letter suggests that he went by the former route. A regular service of passenger "waggons" ran between Burlington and Amboy from 1707. See A. M. Gummere, "Friends in Burlington," *Pennsylvania Magazine* 8 (1884).

**South Carolina, 6, 12, 19, 21–22, 25, 34–37, 39, 42–43, 55, 58, 75**

**South Carolina Gazette, 20–21**

**Southampton Courthouse, 68**
Town in Virginia, now called Courtland and the county town of Southampton County. Several wooden piles very close to the present road bridge seem a likely remnant of the wooden bridge crossed by William Mylne, or a successor to it. It appears that the bridge would have been at least 300 feet long.

**Stephen's Creek (also Stevens Creek), 22, 25, 29–30, 32, 43, 92**
A substantial tributary of the Savannah River on the South Carolina side, joining it about seven miles above Augusta. It has been widened and deepened in recent decades by dams erected on the Savannah. The land on both sides of the Creek is forested, probably as densely as when William lived there, but many of the trees—perhaps thirty to fifty percent—are conifers, which is unlikely to have been the case in the 1770s.

**Strange, Mrs. (Isabella, née Lumisden, later Lady Isabella [d. 1806]), 79**
Wife of Robert Strange. Intellectual, witty, and an effective businesswoman, Mrs. Strange remained a staunch and open supporter of the Stuarts' claim to the British Crown long after other Scots people had abandoned it as a lost cause. See *DNB*.

**Strange, Miss (Mary) Bruce (1748–84), 53, 76, 79**
Friend of Anne Mylne; the eldest daughter of Sir Robert and Lady Isabella Strange and said to have "inherited some of her father's gift." See *DNB*; Mylne Papers, GD1/51, at SRO.

**Strange, Mr. (Robert, later Sir Robert [1721–92]), 49**
A talented draftsman and engraver. He was born Robert Strang in Orkney, fought for Bonnie Prince Charlie in 1745, and engraved his portrait. Strange is believed to have evaded a search party at his fiancée's home by hiding under her hooped skirt. He lived mostly in London but also on the Continent. Having criticized the elitism of the Royal Academy of Arts and

its exclusion of engravers from its membership, he achieved no royal favor until he engraved a picture of the King's children and was knighted in 1787. See *DNB*.

**Stuart, the Honorable John (1718–79),** 23–24, 34–35, 46–47, 53
Son of Bailie (i.e., magistrate) John Steuart, a merchant in Inverness, Scotland, who could claim distant blood relationship with the Pretender to the Scottish throne and had strong, but at times carefully concealed, Jacobite sympathies. The son engaged in commercial ventures in London, Spain, and Charleston with little success. He performed well, however, in social and civic activities but failed to obtain a civil appointment until 1763 when he became superintendent of Indian affairs for the southern colonies, a post created by the British government to "win friends and influence chiefs" among the tribes who occupied land to the west of the white-settled areas, and answering to the British commander-in-chief in the colonies. His salary was initially £600 per annum, raised to £1,000 in 1768, and over ten years he obtained land grants of more than fifteen thousand acres in South Carolina, Georgia, and East Florida and became the owner of two hundred slaves. It was often his task to restrain the greed of colonial governors for more of the tribes' traditional territories. Having suffered from gout since the mid-1760s, in the 1770s he employed two deputies to live in regular contact with the Indians, Alexander Cameron with the Cherokees and David Taitt with the Creeks. He lived at Charleston until the new assembly of South Carolina ordered his arrest in June 1775. He then fled to Saint Augustine and on to Pensacola in July 1776, trying to make the tribes ready to fight on the British side. In 1778 there were several setbacks and he was censured by the British government for these and for a prodigious increase in his expenses. He died at Pensacola in the following year. See *DAB*; Alden, *John Stuart*; Cashin, *The King's Ranger*; Cashin, *Colonial Augusta*.

**Susquehana River (now Susquehanna),** 73
Important navigable river, in Pennsylvania for most of its length but entering the head of Chesapeake Bay in Maryland at a point less than twenty miles south of the Pennsylvania boundary and thirty miles north of Baltimore. Navigation was an obstacle to any plan for bridging it, making the ferries very important for trade.

**Swallow, Mrs.,** 20

**Taitt, David,** 47, 53
A Scotsman trained in mathematics and surveying, appointed as John Stuart's commissary to the Creeks in 1772 and later as deputy superintendent. The appointment ended with Stuart's death in 1779, after which Taitt saw military service at Charleston and Mobile, was imprisoned by the Spanish when Mobile fell in 1780, and when released took ship from Charleston for England in January 1782. See Alden, *John Stuart*, 297; Cashin, *The King's*

*Ranger*; "David Taitt's Journal of a Journey Through the Creek Country, 1772," in Newton D. Mereness, *Travels in the American Colonies* (New York: Antiquarian Press, 1961), 493–565.

**Tarrborough (now Tarboro), 67**
Incorporated as a town at Joseph Howell's Ferry in 1760, although previously a tobacco inspection post and served by a missionary from 1748. It was first planned as a square of five-and-a-half blocks each way. Howell's petition to build a bridge and charge toll was also granted by the Provincial Assembly in 1760. In 1803 the bridge—certainly rebuilt since William Mylne's visit—was described as "five hundred and forty feet long and about thirty feet above the water." See *Rocky Mount Telegram*, Dec. 12, 1967; *Daily Southerner*, Bicentennial edition, July 13, 1976; *Colonial Records of North Carolina*, vol. 6 (1888).

**Tarr River (now Tar River), 67**
A river in North Carolina navigable up to Tarboro and beyond until 1919, at first by "long flat-bottomed boats capable of carrying many barrels of naval stores" (i.e., tar); in the 1890s and after by steam-driven boats. See *Daily Southerner*, Bicentennial edition, July 13, 1976.

**Tea Act, 7, 10**
13 Geo III c 44.

**Three Sisters Ferry, 55**
A public ferry on the Savannah River near modern Clyo and some thirty-five miles upstream from Savannah. See Harper, *Travels of Wm. Bartram*, 381.

**Timothy, Peter, 20**
Son of a French Huguenot printer, protegé of Benjamin Franklin who was cofounder of the *South Carolina Gazette* in 1732. The paper was edited and run by Peter's father, Lewis, from 1733 to his death in 1738, when Peter was thirteen, then by his mother until Peter was old enough to take it over. As owner, editor, and printer, he made it always a beacon of justice, freedom, and independence. In 1781 he was taken prisoner to Saint Augustine and was drowned at sea. See *DAB*; M. Steedman, "Charlestown's Forgotten Tea Party," *Georgia Review* 21, no. 2 (1967).

**Tower Hill, 17**
The Tower of London, first built by William the Conqueror in the eleventh century, stood by the east wall of the city, for protection against attack from the Thames estuary. In the eighteenth century it was still surrounded by a wide moat or ditch filled with water from the Thames. Within the tower were the royal mint, the office of the Crown jewels, and an office of records, as well as military barracks, stores, and state prisons. Between the moat and the city was a wide space known as Tower Hill, used as a place of general resort, as well as for hustings. As a place of execution it saw the last person beheaded

in Britain, the Jacobite Lord Lovat in 1747, but it ceased to be a place of execution after some of the Gordon Rioters were hanged there in 1780. See Maitland, *History of London*, vol. 1, 146–76; Weinreb and Hibbert, *London Encyclopaedia*.

**Trent River,** 67
Tributary of the Neuse River in North Carolina, joining it at New Bern.

**Tryon, Governor (William [1725–88]),** 65, 67
Governor of North Carolina (1765–71) and New York (1771–78). An officer of the Foot Guards from 1752, he married a relative of Lord Hillsborough who in 1763 became first commissioner for trade and plantations in the British government. Tryon was sent to North Carolina as lieutenant-governor in 1764 and became governor a year later. He immediately established the provincial capital at New Bern (see **Tryon's Palace**). He was criticized for neglect of the backcountry. The settlers there banded themselves together under the name of the "Regulators," but Tryon applied a harsh riot act and crushed them by force just before his transfer to New York in 1771. In New York he promoted new settlement to the west and speculated heavily in land himself. He resigned his governorship in 1778 to take up a military command but was sent home to England unfit for service in 1780. He died in London in 1788. See *DAB*; *DNB*; W. S. Powell, ed., *The Correspondence of William Tryon*, 2 vols. (Raleigh, 1980).

**Tryon's Palace,** 65–67
The building called, at first derisively, Tryon's Palace, was built in New Bern, N.C., as a combined governor's residence and seat of government. It was designed by John Hawks and built under his supervision in 1767–71. His several designs show that he modeled it on Nuneham Park, Oxfordshire, in England, designed and built in 1756–64 for Lord Harcourt by Stiff Leadbetter, for whom Hawks had worked. As William Mylne observed, however, some features resembled those of Buckingham House (now Palace), Queen Charlotte's house on the outskirts of London, more than those of Nuneham. Hawks's first design was for a Palladian house of three stories and seven bays, with pavilions of two stories and three bays attached by quadrant passages, all like Nuneham. In the final design the house was reduced to two stories but otherwise similar to Nuneham, while the pavilions were of four bays like Buckingham House. In both designs, and in the house as built, the quadrants were roofed open passages with a colonnade in front and solid rear wall, like those of Buckingham House but unlike Nuneham, where the quadrants were the fronts of solid two-story buildings containing several rooms as well as access corridors to the pavilions. Tryon's Palace was built entirely of brick and roofed with shingles, "a covering," wrote Tryon, "when well executed and painted, more beautiful than slate or tyle." A pediment over the main entrance was occupied by the arms of the king. Rooms in the principal story

were fifteen feet high and those on the bedroom floor twelve feet. They were richly decorated, with fireplaces made of marble from Siena as well as Philadelphia. Skilled workmen were brought from Philadelphia, and a plumber from London. The interior plan closely followed that of Nuneham, with a large entrance hall, two staircases in the middle of the house, and a council chamber thirty-six feet by twenty-two feet as the largest room. There was a formal garden overlooking the Trent river. Tryon and his family moved in in June 1770 and the provincial assembly first met in the council chamber on December 5. The cost of the house, being more than £10,000 sterling and to be raised by a poll tax on the whole province, caused bitter resentment in areas far from the coast and New Bern, a material addition to other grievances that led to bloodshed in the "Regulators" revolt in 1770–71. After the Revolution it was little used; President Washington was entertained to dinner and dancing there in 1791, and thought that it was falling into ruin. In 1798 the main house was gutted by fire. In 1852 both pavilions were standing, but by 1940 only one remained. In the 1950s this pavilion was restored, the rest of the palace rebuilt to the original design, and the gardens also restored. See references under John Hawks. Also see A. T. Dill, *Governor Tryon and His Palace* (Chapel Hill, 1955); W. S. Powell, ed., *The Correspondence of William Tryon*, 2 vols. (Raleigh, 1980); J. Young and T. Lewis, *A Tryon Treasury* (New Bern, 1986); John Hawks's plan of garden (ca. 1770) and memorandum on design of the house (1783), Archivo de Francisco de Miranda, tomo 5, ff. 95–97, Academia Nacional de la Historia, Caracas, Venezuela; John Hawks plans, Colonial Office papers, PRO; Colen Campbell et al, *Vitruvius Britannicus*, vol. 1 (London, 1715), plates 43–44, and vol. 5 (London, 1771), plates 99–100; H. M. Colvin, ed., *History of the King's Works*, vol. 5 (London, 1976), 133–38, and plates 5–7.

**Virginia,** 26, 55, 68, 72–73, 75

**Waiscoat, Daniel,** 46, 60
House carpenter in Augusta. Signed the Loyalist resolution in Saint Paul's Parish, published on October 12, 1774.

**Wapping,** 16
In the eighteenth century, a village just to the east of London on the north side of the Thames and employed solely in service to the maritime trade of the port.

**West End, London,** 15
In the eighteenth century the city's west end was at about Ludgate Hill just west of Saint Paul's Cathedral. Today's West End is a theater district a mile further west and quite outside the small area that is still administered as the City of London.

**Westminster Bridge,** 16
The stone bridge built in 1735–50 at Westminster, the seat of government of Great Britain, one mile up the Thames from the City of London. It was

the first large "modern" bridge in Britain and considered one of the finest in Europe. Designed and directed by engineer Charles Labelye, a Frenchman born in Switzerland. See Ruddock, *Arch Bridges*.

**Whitby**, 36–37

**Williams, Mrs.** (Catherine Chilcott), 50, 60
Daughter of Mary Malbone Chilcott (later Mary Mackay) of Rhode Island. Catherine married John Francis Williams about 1769 and went to live at Augusta. She was separated from him before his death in 1775 and lived with her mother and stepfather, Robert Mackay. She later married Andrew McLean, a merchant in Augusta and business associate of Robert Mackay. McLean died in 1784. Catherine married John Course, a lawyer in Augusta, in 1789. For references, see **Mackay, Mary**.

**Williams, John Francis** (d. 1775), 46
Trader and/or merchant in Augusta, probably from before 1756. His partnership with Robert Mackay was dissolved in June 1770. He married Catherine Chilcott about 1769. He was later described by Mackay as a "strange mortal" and fraudulent in business. He died while at Savannah in January 1775 to prove the debts due to him from the Indian nations, before payment by the provincial government. For references, see **Mackay, Mary**. Also see Cashin, *Colonial Augusta*.

**Williamsburgh (now Williamsburg)**, 68–69, 71–72, 75
Provincial capital of Virginia planned by Lieutenant-Governor Francis Nicholson in 1699 on a site of 220 acres. He chose a regular layout and generous space standards, with each individual building lot of half an acre for a house and garden. The central street (Duke of Gloucester Street) was ninety-nine feet wide. In 1782 many lots were still empty but the southern half of the street, from Market Square to the Capitol, was fully built up. The rebuilt capitol, finished in 1933, is a replica of the one built in 1701–5 and destroyed by fire in 1747; but the provision of rooms and their positions in the building are much the same as those of the later capitol described by William Mylne. The second capitol was raised on the foundations of the first, with the same H-shaped plan. The two-story portico mentioned by Mylne had the king's arms carved in wood in the pediment, but the rebels took them down and burned them in or before 1777. See M. Whiffen, *Public Buildings of Williamsburg* (New York: 1958); *Colonial Williamsburg: Official Guidebook* (1979); H. Jones, *The Present State of Virginia* (London, 1724).

**Williamson, Mr.**, 43–44
Almost certainly Andrew Williamson (ca. 1730–86), a planter at White Hall in South Carolina, six miles west of Ninety-Six and perhaps fifteen miles east of the Savannah River. Williamson contracted with Lieutenant-Governor Bull in 1765 to erect Fort Charlotte. He became an officer of the rebel militia early in the Revolution and was quickly promoted by steps to brigadier-general. After commanding a force of up to two thousand South Carolinians

for several years, he withdrew his militia of about 360 men from Augusta into South Carolina in May 1780, a few weeks before Thomas Brown reoccupied the town for the Crown. In June Williamson surrendered to a Royalist officer at Ninety-Six. He was suspected of conniving with the enemy and was rescued from hanging only by the protection of British troops, but he later cleared his name sufficiently to remain in South Carolina to the end of his life. He was clearly an officer of humanitarian principles, having banned all revenge and looting when his force entered Augusta in February 1779, and also protected James Gordon from "persecution," probably for several years. See *DAB*; Cashin and Robertson, *Augusta and the American Revolution*; Cashin, *The King's Ranger*; Alden, *History of the American Revolution*.

**"Willy" (or "Will"), 18, 26, 40, 45, 53, 77, 79, 84**
William Mylne's illegitimate son.

**Wilmington, 64–65, 67**
Seaport town of North Carolina, on the north, or east, side of the Cape Fear River. The original street plan was a chessboard of streets parallel and perpendicular to the riverfront. The central perpendicular street was Market, and a map drawn in 1769 showed only one block completed on each side of Market Street, with others partly built. See Plan of Wilmington, 1769, by C. J. Saulthier, British Library, London; drawing by T. E. Hyde, 1826, Wilmington Public Library.

**Wilson, Captain, 12**
Probably James Wilson, master of the ship *Portland*, which reached Charleston one day before the *London* in December 1773. See *South Carolina Gazette*, Dec. 6, 1773.

**Wilson, John, 9**
Overseer of the repair and completion of North Bridge, Edinburgh, from 1770 to 1775.

**Wright, Sir James, Baronet (1716–85), 6, 34–36, 46–47, 53, 56**
Last royal governor of Georgia, 1761–82. Born in London, son of a chief justice of South Carolina, he was attorney-general of that province by 1739 and later became its agent in London. In 1760 he was appointed lieutenant-governor and in 1761 governor of Georgia. His attempts, from 1774 onward, to restrain the patriotic movement failed, and after a period of imprisonment in his own house, he escaped to a warship in February 1776 and sailed to England. When Savannah was taken by British troops in 1778, he returned and tried to govern the province until he was ordered home in 1782. For the loss of his property, which had been confiscated in 1778 and was valued at £33,000, he was given a pension of £500 per annum. He died in Westminster, where he was buried in the north cloister of the abbey. See *DNB*; AO 12 and 13, at PRO, London.

**Wrightsborough,** 38, 43, 46
A township in Northeastern Georgia touching on the boundary of white settlement set by the Proclamation of 1763, in the angle between the Little River and Williams Creek. Wrightsborough, which was named for the governor, Sir James Wright, was established in 1768 by a group of fifty Quaker families who came from North Carolina, just the sort of disciplined settlers the governor wanted. Its population was at least six hundred by 1775. See De Vorsey, *The Indian Boundary*.

CPSIA information can be obtained
at www.ICGtesting.com
Printed in the USA
BVHW071418220921
617257BV00007B/158